ABORTION
IS A SATANIC SACRIFICE

ABORTION
IS A SATANIC SACRIFICE

The CD Transcript

Zachary King

MCP BOOKS

MCP Books
2301 Lucien Way #415
Maitland, FL 32751
407-339-4217

Printed in the United States of America

Bible quotes used in these discs are from the Knox translation

Edited by Alex Sperle

ISBN: 9781545613122

Special thanks to :
The Blessed Mother, Queen of Heaven and Earth
St. Faustina, Blessed Bartolo Longo
Sister Mary Crown of Purity.

Prayer to St Michael

Saint Michael the Archangel, defend us in battle. Be our protection against the wickedness and snares of the devil. May God rebuke him, we humbly pray. And do thou, O Prince of the Heavenly Hosts, by the power of God, thrust into hell satan, and all evil spirits who prowl about the world seeking the ruin of souls.

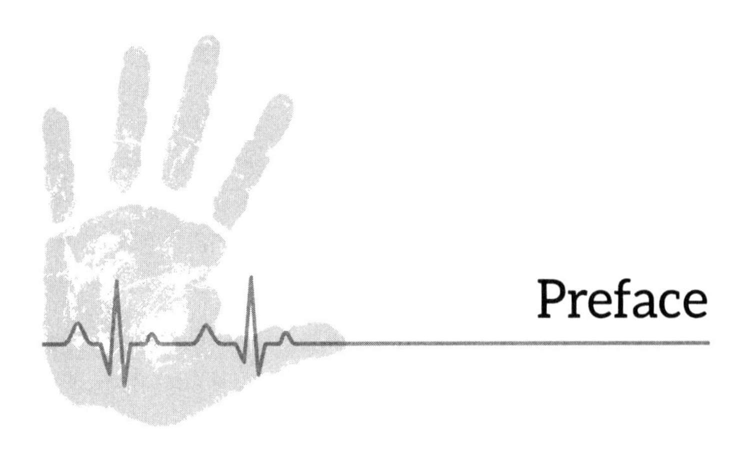

Preface

I am hoping that everyone reading this has listened to the CD set. This is a direct transcript from the CD set. You may notice some errors if you go back and listen to the CD's you'll notice the errors are there as well. The CD set was professionally done and yet we still missed some stuff. But I did not wish to change the transcript in those ways. I want you to be able to follow along with the CD set if you so desire. The differences, because there are a couple, is this preface that you are reading, and three observations at the end of the transcript and a reference letter from Fr Frank Pavone. Those three observations I wanted to put into the CD set, but we thought the set sounded "nicer" without them. But I have been told by multiple people that I should have included them. So here they are.

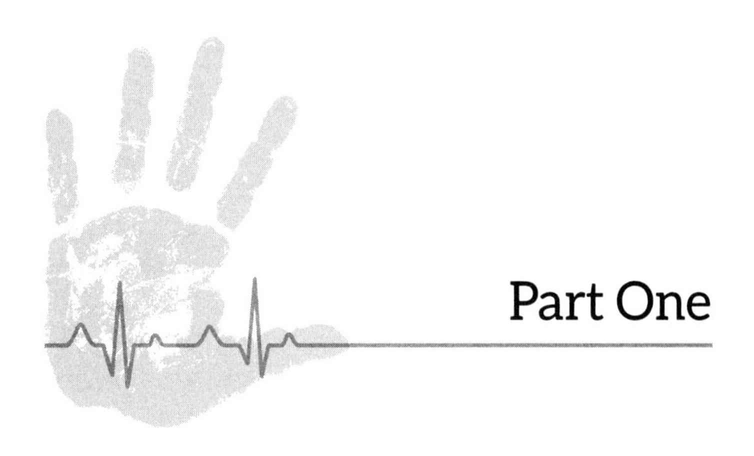

Part One

Written and edited by Zachary and Katie King
Read by: Katie King

Due to the possible graphic nature in the content of this CD parental guidance is suggested. To some this information will not be graphic at all and to others it will be horrific. It is no more disturbing than watching CNN after 9 pm but even that content could be too strong for some listeners.

Use your best judgment when listening to it or playing it for others. Remember who's in the room or in ear shot when playing.

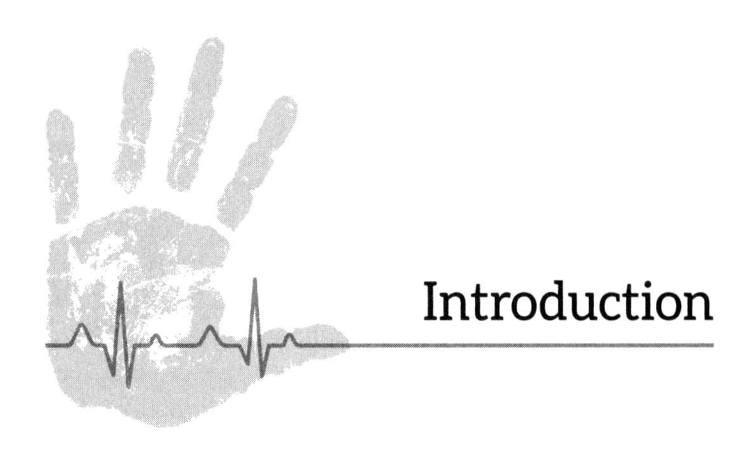

Introduction

Romans 14:7-9 & 12

7 None of us lives as his own master, and none of us dies as his own master. 8 While we live, we live as the Lord's servants, when we die, we die as the Lord's servants; in life and in death, we belong to the Lord. 9 That was why Christ died and lived again; he would be Lord both of the dead and of the living. and so each of us will have to give an account of himself before God.

In the bible the Greek word "Pharmakia" is translated into the word "Sorcery" and on Tuesday July 16th 2013 in a Catholic Answers Open Forum regarding the bible verses Revelations 9:21 where it says, "and they did not repent of their murders nor of their sorceries nor of their immorality nor of their thefts." And in Galatians 5:19-20 when Paul states, "Now the deeds of the flesh are evident, which are: immorality, impurity, sensuality, idolatry, sorcery, enmities, strife, jealousy, outbursts of anger, disputes, dissensions, factions, envying, drunkenness, carousing, and things like these, of which I forewarn you, just as I have forewarned you, that those who practice such things will not inherit the kingdom of God." Tim Staples mentioned that in the very early centuries of the church the word "pharmakia" is used referring to a terrible concoction that was given to women to induce Abortion, which would also often kill the mother. He also mentions that many scholars believe that in these biblical verses where "pharmakia" is used it is in reference to these abortifacients.

In The Examination of Conscience from Ignatius Press

Mortal sins listed under the commandment

"Thou Shall Not Kill"

- Unjust killing, murder
- Abortion
- Counseling a woman to have an abortion or assisting in an abortion; participation in surrogate motherhood;
- Artificial insemination; participation in sperm banks;
- Obtaining surgery for the intended purpose of sterilization;
- Mutilation of the body

- Attempted suicide;
- Violent behavior
- Needlessly putting your life or the life of another in danger (eg: reckless driving); physically fighting or striking another;
- Excessive drinking of alcoholic beverages or excessive smoking;
- Abusive use of prescribed drugs;
- Using, distributing, or selling illegal drugs
- Too much or too little sleeping or eating (eg: laziness, gluttony, wasting one's time, vain preoccupation about diet)
- Not taking reasonable care of one's health; excessive concern over bodily health or appearance;
- Taking revenge;
- Anger, hatred, aversion, coldness, or resentment toward another;
- Name calling or abusive or harsh language toward another; rude or impolite conduct; inconsideration for the feelings of others;
- Mocking the physically or mentally handicapped or those of another race or religion;
- Giving bad example for others to imitate;
- Lack of compassion for someone afflicted;
- Failing to help another in danger or serious necessity;
- Boasting of one's accomplishments;

- Stubbornness in one's opinions;
- Favoring opinions contrary to Church teaching;
- Impatience
- Cruel treatment of animals.

This CD is being brought to you by All Saints Ministry. My name is Zachary King in a nut shell I was a Satanist and involved in new age practices for 26+ years. I was brought to Jesus by His Mother through the power of the Miraculous Medal in January 2008 and I have been fighting evil ever since. Thank you for listening to this disc and may the peace of the Lord always be with you.

I know many of you don't wish to hear a story this abominable. Even just saying the word 'abortion' is too strong of language for some. But entertaining this thought as well... guess who else doesn't want this story told? Because if we kept these images under a rock and didn't let them out into the light,

Abortion will never go away. There are people that think abortion is a woman's choice but have no idea how one is performed.

In this CD you will learn why they're performed. And how. The next time someone tells you that abortion is a simple, painless procedure then you can take them to task. After listening to this CD you'll know the seven ways there are to get an abortion and that none of them are simple, safe, or painless.

To some, the information I present here will be old hat. A lot of you listening will know Margaret Sangers name and her history. But some will be hearing this for the first time. So even if you think you know everything I'm saying, at least the 1st time you listen, please don't skip ahead.

I pray this becomes your most listened to and shared CD.

There is a full history of Margaret Sanger's life. There are multiple books and tons of info on the internet. We will only be looking at the highlights and a smattering of her quotes. This CD, after all, is about abortion being a satanic sacrifice, not about Ms Sanger. She plays but a role in this heinous history of satanic death.

Keep in mind as well that since this information is from Wikipedia or other online sources the exact quote is subject to change, though the information is confirmed

Margret Higgens Sanger was born in September 14th, 1879 and died September 6th, 1966 she was an American birth control activist, sex educator, and nurse. Sanger popularized the term 'birth control', opened the first birth control clinic in the United States and established Planned Parenthood.

Her mother, Anne Purcell Higgins was a devout Catholic who went through 18 pregnancies with 11 live births in 22 years before dying at age 50 of Tuberculosis and Cervical cancer. Margaret's father Michael Hennesy Higgins was a Catholic who became an atheist and an activist for women's suffrage and free public education.

-Wikipedia

In 1911 Sanger started writing articles in magazines espousing her radical views.

Sanger went to school, graduated and became a nurse in 1912.

In 1913 Sanger worked as a nurse at Henry street settlement in New York's lower east side, often with poor women who were suffering due to frequent child birth and self-induced abortions. Searching for something that would help these women, Sanger visited public libraries but was unable to find information on contraception. These problems were optimized in a story that sanger would later recount in her speeches; while Sanger was working as a nurse She was called to Sadie Sachs apartment after Sach's had become extremely ill due to a self-induced abortion. Afterward Sadie begged the attending doctor to tell her how she could prevent this from happening again to which the doctor simply gave the advice to remain abstinent. A few months later Sanger was once again called back to the Sach's apartment, only this time Sadie was found dead after yet another self-induced abortion. Sanger would sometimes end the story by saying, "I threw my nursing bag in the corner and announced that I would never take another case until I had made it possible for working women in America to have the knowledge to control birth." Although Sadie Sachs was possibly a fictional composite of several women Sanger had known, this story marks the time when Sanger began to devote her life to help desperate women before they were driven to pursue dangerous and illegal abortions.

-Wikipedia

Sanger was indicted in august 1914 on 3 counts of violating obscenity laws and a fourth count of inciting murder and assassination. Fearing that she might be sent to prison without an opportunity to argue for birth control in court she fled to England under the alias Bertha Watson, during her self-imposed exile her views gained popularity in the United States. She returned and the charges were dropped in early 1916.

- On October 16th 1916 Sanger opened a family planning and birth control clinic in Brooklyn. Nine days later she was arrested for distributing contraceptives.
- January 1917 she was convicted and sentenced to 30 days.

After a 1918 court ruling that exempted physicians from the law that prohibited the distribution of contraceptive information to women—provided it was prescribed for medical reasons—she established the Clinical Research Bureau (CRB) in 1923 to exploit this loophole.[7][29] The CRB was the first legal birth control clinic in the United States, and it was staffed entirely by female doctors and social workers.[30] The clinic received a large amount of funding from John D. Rockefeller Jr. and his family, which continued to make donations to Sanger's causes in future decades, but generally made them anonymously to avoid public exposure of the family name.

John D. Rockefeller Jr. donated five thousand dollars to her American Birth Control League in 1924 and a second time in 1925.

In 1939 two organizations Margaret belonged to the ABCL and the BBCRD merged to become the Birth Control Federation of America. In 1942 they changed their name to Planned Parenthood.

Sanger encouraged philanthropist Catherine McCormick to provide funding for biologist Gregory Pincus to develop the birth control pill. In 1946 Sanger helped planned parenthood go global.

Margaret then took the role of President and held it until she was 80 years old. Sanger died of congestive heart failure at the age of 86 in 1966.

**The year I was born. **

There are movies and books about Sangers life and her writings are curated by two universities: New York University, and Smith College.

In 1957 The American Humanist Association named her 'humanist of the year'.

There is a residential building on stony brook university campus with her name on it. And a room in the Wellesley Colleges library and Margaret Sanger Square in New York city's Greenwich Village.

In 1993 the Margaret Sanger Clinic where she provided birth control services in NY in the mid 20th century was designated as a national historic landmark by the National Park Service.

In 1966 Planned Parenthood began issuing the Margaret Sanger awards annually to honor "individuals of distinction in recognition of excellence and leadership in furthering reproductive health and reproductive rights."

In a few minutes, I will present the list of all Margaret Sanger awards recipients from 1966-2015.

Sanger was a proponent of negative eugenics, which aims to improve human hereditary traits through social intervention by reducing reproduction by those considered unfit. She also recommended that immigration exclude those "whose condition is known to be detrimental to the stamina of the race" and that sterilization and segregation be applied to those with incurable hereditary disabilities.

Sanger believed that lighter skinned races were superior to darker skinned races.

Margaret Sanger believed the only way to change the law was to break it.

Margaret Sanger believed her mother died from so many pregnancies.

-pbs.org

1939 Margaret Sanger said "we should hire 3 or 4 colored ministers preferably with social service back grounds and with engaging personalities... we don't want the word to get out that we want to exterminate the negro population."

Sanger broadly supported the Eugenics movement, advocating for a superior race that was free of poor, immigrant, and minority citizens. She even spoke at a rally of the Klu Klux Klan. Despite this evidence, Planned Parenthood, the nation's leading abortion provider, has done little to distance itself from Sanger's legacy."

Some quotes of Margaret Sanger illustrate her attitudes towards race and eugenics,

> "We do not want word to go out that we want to exterminate the Negro

> population, and the minister is the man who can straighten out that idea if it ever occurs to any of their more rebellious members" (Sanger's letter to Clarence J. Gamble, 1939, December)

Margaret Sanger referred to immigrants and Catholics as reckless breeders, writing in her book, Pivot of Civilization, "[They're] an unceasingly spawning class of human beings who never should have been born at all." (Sanger, p.187).

"The most merciful thing that a large family does to one of its infant members is to kill it," Margaret Sanger wrote in her 1920 book Women and the New Race (Sanger, p. 63).

In a 1921 article in the Birth Control Review Sanger wrote, "the most urgent problem today is how to limit and discourage the over fertility of the mentally and physically Defective." The viewers of one of her 1919 articles interpreted her objectives as, "more children from the fit, less from the unfit" again the question of who decides fitness is important and it was an issue that Sanger only partly addressed, "the undeniably feeble minded should indeed not only be discouraged but prevented from propagating their kind".

-Black genocide.org

"Our failure to segregate morons who are increasing and multiplying... demonstrates our foolhardy and extravagant sentimentalism" she wrote in the recently republished THE PIVOT OF CIVILIZATION. This book written in 1922 was published at a time when scientific racism had been used to assert black inferiority. Who determines who is a moron? How would these morons be segregated? The ramifications of such statements are bone chilling.

-Black genocide.org

An overview and more quotes from Margaret Sanger.

On sterilization & racial purification:

Sanger believed that, for the purpose of racial "purification," couples should be rewarded who chose sterilization. Birth Control in America, The Career of Margaret Sanger, by David Kennedy, p. 117, quoting a 1923 Sanger speech.

On the right of married couples to bear children:

Couples should be required to submit applications to have a child, she wrote in her "Plan for Peace." Birth Control Review, April 1932.

On the purpose of birth control:

The purpose in promoting birth control was "to create a race of thoroughbreds," she wrote in the Birth Control Review, Nov. 1921 (p. 2)

On the rights of the handicapped and mentally ill, and racial minorities:

"More children from the fit, less from the unfit -- that is the chief aim of birth control." Birth Control Review, May 1919, p. 12.

On eradicating 'bad stocks':

The goal of eugenicists is "to prevent the multiplication of bad stocks," wrote Dr. Ernst Rudin in the April 1933 Birth Control Review (of which Sanger was editor). Another article exhorted Americans to "restrict the propagation of those physically, mentally and socially inadequate."

One of Sanger's greatest influences, sexologist/ eugenicist Dr. Havelock Ellis (with whom she had an affair, leading to her divorce from her first husband), urged mandatory sterilization of the poor as a prerequisite to receiving any public aid. The Problem of Race Regeneration, by Havelock Ellis, p. 65.

Birth control as an economic improvement measure had some appeal to those lowest on the income ladder. In the black Chicago Defender for January 10th

1942 a long 3 column womans interest article discussed the endorsement of the Sanger Program by prominent black women. There were at least 6 express references, such as the following example, to birth control as a remedy for economic woes: "It raised the standard of living by enabling parents to adjust the family size to the family income." Readers were also told that birth control, "is no operation. It is no abortion. Abortion kills life after it has begun… birth control is neither harmful nor immoral."

-Black Genocide.org

Hillary Clinton receives award named for famed eugenicist.

When former secretary of state Hillary Clinton received Planned Parenthoods highest honor it came in the name of a woman who promoted eliminating the 'unfit' from the human race. The Planned Parenthood federation of America presented Clinton with the Margaret Sanger award at its annual awards dinner March 27th 2009 in Houston Texas. Sanger founded an organization in 1916 that eventually became Planned Parenthood. Receiving the award is 'a great privilege' Clinton said after the presentation "I admire Margaret Sanger enormously, her courage, her tenacity, her vision… I am really in awe of her".

Since taking office Obama has reversed the Mexico City policy which barred federal funds from organizations that promote or perform abortions overseas. He also has restored money through the state department to the UNFPA, or United Nations population fund which had its congressional funding withdrawn by the bush administration for 7 years for its apparent support of Chinas coercive population control program.

In her speech Clinton said she is very proud when Obama struck down the Mexico City policy, she also was pleased to tell the Planned Parenthood audience the administration would fund UNFPA. Secretary of state assured the abortion rights advocates that, "reproductive rights and the umbrella issue of women's rights and empowerment will be a key to the foreign policy of this administration."

Access to abortion is part of "reproductive rights" in the terminology of Planned Parenthood and its allies. The international Planned Parenthood federation another organization Sanger founded was one of the beneficiaries of Obamas repeal of the Mexico City policy.

-ERLC.com (ethics and religious liberty commission)

**If morality right and wrong or God and the devil didn't enter this equation or if we didn't look at the lives of children being destroyed then maybe… just maybe we could go along with Ms Sanger or at least some of her ideas. But when you look at her in the big picture it's quite a disturbing painting indeed. At the very least she was racist. But she had major ties to the Ku Klux Klan and Nazi Germany. She started an organization that would later become Planned Parenthood and would become responsible for more deaths than Adolf Hitler. And this is who Hillary Rodham Clinton holds in awe and admires. **.

The Margaret Sanger award has been given out to recipients since 1966. The award can be declined by anyone who might be offended by such an award but no one has ever rejected it. This disc is being made in 2015 Let's take a look at its 49 recipients and see if we know any of them or have ever heard of them.

You'll notice some years have multiple recipients (I don't think anyone who receives this award could be called a winner- this is more like a dubious honor. Kind of like satan is saying you're good at something)

1966
The Reverend Martin Luther King Jr.
General William H. Draper
Carl G. Hartman, MD
President Lyndon Baines Johnson

Seems such an atrocity that a president would be eligible for such an award and to make it worse, he accepted. Strange that President Obama has not won this award yet. That's disgraceful on so many levels.

1967
John D. Rockefeller III
I guess you can only donate large amounts of money to them for so long till they give you something back.

1968
The Honorable Ernest Gruening
This is the 1st in a slew of judges to receive this heinous award.

1969
Hugh Mackintosh Foot

1970
The Honorable Joseph D. Tydings

1971
Louis M. Hellman, MD

1972
Alan F. Guttmacher, MD

1973
Sarah Lewit Tietze and Christopher Tietze, MD

1974
Harriet F. Pilpel, JD

1975
Cass Canfield

1976
John Rock, MD

1977
Bernard Berelson, PhD

1978
Julia Henderson
Frederick S. Jaffe
Edris Rice-Wray, MD, PhD

1979
Alfred E. Moran
The Honorable Robert Packwood

1980
Mary S. Calderone, MD
Sarah Weddington, Esq.

1981
The Honorable William G. Milliken

1982
Madame Jihan Sadat

1983
Katharine Hepburn
Yes it is THE Katherine Hepburn. In 1981 Ms. Hepburn wrote a fundraising letter for Planned Parenthood that helped raise $1 Million for them. Katherines Mother, named Katherine Houghten Hepburn had actually worked years before with Margaret Sanger to start Planned Parenthood.
By the way all the information I'm presenting here about the winners of the Margaret Sanger award recipients can be found at the Planned Parenthood website.
Finishing up with Katherine Hepburn, in 1988 Planned Parenthood established the Katherine Houghten Hepburn Fund to honor the mother and daughter.
How sweet.

1984
Bishop Paul Moore
Who thankfully was Episcopal and not Catholic. He was a social justice priest as well and advocated for the ordination of women and ordained the 1st lesbian Episcopal Priest.

1985
Guadalupe de la Vega
Mechai Viravaidya

1986
Jeannie I. Rosoff

1987
Phil Donahue
Yep, the day time talk show guy. He is very liberal and often featured liberal vs conservative issues such as abortion on his show. He considers himself Roman Catholic.

1988
Ann Landers
Abigail Van Buren
Ann Landers began writing her advice column under her own name in 1955 and Abigail began her Dear Abby column soon after.
What a shame to have two people who could influence so many people in a positive way instead promote something so intrinsically evil.

1989
Henry Morgentaler, MD

1990
Mufaweza Khan

1991
The Honorable Bella Abzug

1992
Faye Wattleton

1993
Richard Steele, Audrey Steele Burnand, Barbara Steele Williams

1994
Fred Sai

1995
Jane Hodgson, MD

1996
Justice Harry A. Blackmun

1997
Louise Tyrer, MD
Robin Chandler Duke

1998
The Reverend Howard Moody
Not associated with The Moody Bible Institute, this Rev. Moody was Church of Christ and a Baptist Minister. He was a contributor to Religious Coalition for Reproductive Choice and a vocal advocate of abortion.

2000
Nafis Sadik, MD

2001
Kathleen Turner
Another actress. She is the Chair Person of the American Board of Advocates for Planned Parenthood.

2003
Jane Fonda
Funny it seems like she would have won sooner. She donated $1.3 million to an Atlanta Georgia Hospital to pay for teenagers to get abortions.

2004
Ted Turner
Forum for Women, Law, and Development of Nepal
The billionaire behind Turner broadcasting has started and funded many abortion groups including one with an extremely shameful name, Catholics for a Free Choice.

He also donated $1 billion to help fund one of these abortion and "birth control" organizations.

2005
Gloria Feldt

2006
Karen Pearl
Allan Rosenfield, MD

2007
Dolores Huerta

2008
Kenneth C. Edelin, MD

2009
U.S. Secretary of State Hillary Rodham Clinton

2010
Ellen R. Malcolm

2011
Anthony D. Romero

2012
Philip Darney, MD, MSc and Uta Landy, PhD

2013
Famed sex therapist and media personality
Dr. Ruth K. Westheimer

2014
Nancy Pelosi

In 2014 Nancy Pelosi spoke at a planned parenthood gala stating that abortion opponents are closed minded, oblivious, and dumb. Interesting that as a self proclaimed Roman Catholic that she speak that way about the pope.

Some random quotes from Planned Parenthood:

From a pamphlet called "If you've had an abortion"

"Abortion is a common experience for women and girls nationwide".

"Did you know over one third of women in the US will have an abortion by age 45"

"Women of all ages, races, economic backgrounds and religions and religious beliefs have abortions"

"1.3 million abortions happen in the United States every year"

"The life time average is about one abortion per woman world wide"

From a pamphlet called "We Believe"

Under the topic "Sexuality"

"Abstinence only programs are inadequate to ensure sexual health"

But under "Expression" it says

"Abstaining from sexual intercourse is the most effective method of preventing pregnancy and sexually transmitted infections"

Under "Love" it says

"60% of the pregnancies in this country are unintended"

And back to "Expression" we learn

"Becoming a sexually healthy adult is an important part of adolescent development"

Sounds like satans in charge of Planned Parenthood

From the pamphlet "This is Planned Parenthood"

They allege their 129 affiliates operate 875 local health centers across the United States.

And further down the page it says,

"For almost 30 years Family Planning International Assistance, the International Service Division of Planned Parenthood, has provided critical family planning, education and services to 70 countries".

According to a pamphlet titled "Medication Abortion"

"Like all medical procedures, medication abortion carries some risk. But it is much safer than childbirth" (So killing the baby is safer than letting it live).

A little further down it states:

"Most women ultimately feel relief after abortion. Some women feel anger, regret, guilt or sadness for a little while."

"Serious long term emotional problems after abortion are as uncommon as they are after childbirth".

In a pamphlet titled "In Clinic Abortion" we read

"Abortion in the first 20 weeks of pregnancy is much safer than childbirth".

All the different types of abortions offered by planned parenthood for in clinic take between 5 and 20 minutes to do and recovery time is about an hour... unless you get some of those random guilt, anger or regret feelings that happen as often as they do in childbirth.

If you did not know how an abortion happens before listening to this CD you'll have no doubt by the end.

So how do abortions happen? I know there are some out there that still don't have a clue as to how they happen at a doctor's office or planned parenthood. There seems to be this misconception that the woman takes a pill and then she is magically not pregnant anymore. Or the doctor performs some procedure and the pregnancy is terminated. They use such colorful phrasing. "The pregnancy is terminated" doesn't that sound a lot nicer than "The baby is dead".

Let's examine how many types of abortions there are and see how each is done. This information can be found at LifeSiteNews.com.

The following will be a graphic description of abortion, if this is too difficult to listen to, feel free to fast forward.

Surgical Abortions

There are many methods of abortion. The procedure used depends largely upon the stage of pregnancy and the size of the unborn child. Dr. J.C. Willke, in his book, Abortion: Questions and Answers (Hayes Publishing Co. Inc, Cincinnati, 1985), has divided the methods of abortion into three main categories: those that invade the uterus and kill the child by instruments which enter the uterus through the cervix; those that kill the preborn child by administration of drugs and then induce labor and the delivery of a dead baby; and, those that invade the uterus by abdominal surgery.

Dilation of the uterus is required in cervical methods of abortion. The usual method of dilation is to insert a series of instruments of increasing size into the cervix. A set of dilators, metallic curved instruments, are used to open the cervix sufficiently to accommodate the instruments of abortion. In contrast with a normal birth, where the dilation occurs slowly over a period of many hours, the forceful stretching by the abortionist to open the cervix takes a matter of seconds. This premature and unnatural stretching of the cervix can result in permanent physical injury to the mother.

Laminaria (dehydrated material, usually seaweed) is sometimes used to reduce damage to the cervix. Inserted into the cervix the day before the scheduled abortion, it absorbs water and swells, gradually pushing open the cervix in the process.

Eight-week pre-born baby

At eight to nine weeks the eyelids have begun forming and hair appears. By the ninth and tenth weeks the preborn child sucks her thumb, turns somersaults, jumps, can squint to close out light, frown, swallow, and move her tongue.

At this early stage of development, suction abortions are performed using a smaller tube, requiring little dilation of the cervix. This is called "menstrual extraction." However, if all the fetal remains are not removed, infection results, requiring full dilation of the cervix and a scraping out of the womb.

Suction Aspiration

Suction Aspiration This is the most common method of abortion during the first 12 weeks of pregnancy. General or local anesthesia is given to the mother and her cervix is quickly dilated. A suction curette (hollow tube with a knife-edged tip) is inserted into the womb. This instrument is then connected to a vacuum machine by a transparent tube. The vacuum suction, 29 times more powerful than a household vacuum cleaner, tears the fetus and placenta into small pieces which are sucked through the tube into a bottle and discarded.

Dilation and Curettage (D&C)

This method is similar to the suction method with the added insertion of a hook shaped knife (curette) which cuts the baby into pieces. The pieces are scraped out through the cervix and discarded. [Note: This abortion method should not be confused with a therapeutic D&C done for reasons other than pregnancy.]

12 Weeks

By the end of the third month all arteries are present, including the coronary vessels of the heart. Blood is circulating through these vessels to all body parts.

The heart beat ranges during this fetal period from 110 to 160 beats per minute. All blood cells are produced by the liver and spleen, a job soon taken over by the bone marrow. White blood cells, important for immunity, are formed in the lymph nodes and thymus.

Vocal chords are complete, and the child can and does sometimes cry (silently). The brain is fully formed, and the child can feel pain. The fetus may even suck his thumb. The eyelids now cover the eyes, and will remain shut until the seventh month to protect the delicate optical nerve fibers.
14 weeks: Muscles lengthen and become organized. The mother will soon start feeling the first flutters of the baby kicking and moving inside.

15 weeks: The fetus has an adult's taste buds and may be able to savor the mother's meals.

16 weeks: Five and a half inches tall and only six ounces in weight, eyebrows, eyelashes and fine hair appear. The child can grasp with his hands, kick, or even somersault.

Eighteen week pre-born baby

The fetus is now about 5 inches long. The child blinks, grasps, and moves her mouth. Hair grows on the head and body.

20 weeks: The child can hear and recognize mother's voice. Though still small and fragile, the baby is growing rapidly and could possibly survive if born at this stage. Fingernails and fingerprints appear. Sex

organs are visible. Using an ultrasound device, the doctor can tell if the child is a girl or a boy.

Dilation and Evacuation (D&E)

This method is used up to 18 weeks' gestation. Instead of the loop-shaped knife used in D&C abortions, a pair of forceps is inserted into the womb to grasp part of the fetus. The teeth of the forceps twist and tear the bones of the unborn child. This process is repeated until the fetus is totally dismembered and removed. Usually the spine must be snapped and the skull crushed in order to remove them.

Salt Poisoning (Saline Injection):

Saline Injection Used after 16 weeks (four months) when enough fluid has accumulated. A long needle injects a strong salt solution through the mother's abdomen into the baby's sac. The baby swallows this fluid and is poisoned by it. It also acts as a corrosive, burning off the outer layer of skin. It normally takes somewhat over an hour for the baby to die from this. Within 24 hours, labor will usually set in and the mother will give birth to a dead or dying baby. (There have been many cases of these babies being born alive. They are usually left unattended to die. However, a few have survived and later been adopted.)

Six month pre-born baby

The unborn child is covered with a fine, downy hair called lanugo. Its tender skin is protected by a waxy substance called vernix. Some of this substance may still be on the child's skin at birth at which time it will be quickly absorbed. The child practices breathing by inhaling amniotic fluid into developing lungs.

Prostaglandin Chemical Abortion

Prostaglandin Abortion This form of abortion uses chemicals developed by the Upjohn Pharmaceutical Co. which cause the uterus to contract intensely, pushing out the developing baby. The contractions are more violent than normal, natural contractions, so the unborn baby is frequently killed by them -- some have even been decapitated. Many, however, have also been born alive.

Hysterectomy or Caesarean Section

Used mainly in the last three months of pregnancy, the womb is entered by surgery through the wall of the abdomen. The technique is similar to a Caesarean delivery, except that the umbilical cord is usually cut while the baby is still in the womb, thus cutting off his oxygen supply and causing him to suffocate. Sometimes the baby is removed alive and simply left in a corner to die of neglect or exposure.

Eight month pre-born baby At 30 Weeks

For several months, the umbilical cord has been the baby's lifeline to the mother. Nourishment is transferred from the mother's blood, through the placenta, and into the umbilical cord to the fetus. If the mother ingests any toxic substances, such as drugs or alcohol, the baby receives these as well.

32 weeks: The fetus sleeps 90-95% of the day, and sometimes experiences REM sleep, an indication of dreaming.

Partial-Birth Abortion

These are supposed to be illegal but do occur

Five steps to a partial birth abortion:

- Partial Birth Abortion Guided by ultrasound, the abortionist grabs the baby's legs with forceps.
- The baby's leg is pulled out into the birth canal.
- The abortionist delivers the baby's entire body, except for the head.

- Partial Birth Abortion The abortionist jams scissors into the baby's skull. The scissors are then opened to enlarge the skull.
- The scissors are removed and a suction catheter is inserted. The child's brains are sucked out, causing the skull to collapse. The dead baby is then removed.

When speaking at a Planned Parenthood gathering before his election President Obama said "the first thing I'd do as president is sign the freedom of choice act. That's the first thing I'd do." That means he promised, that his first act as president would be to bring back partial birth abortions and make them legal for any age female to obtain and underage girls would not need parental consent. While we are on the subject of president Obama he voted to legalize late term abortions. Late term abortions are particularly controversial, as the baby is more developed and can often survive outside of the womb.

He voted to legalize late term abortions in Illinois. And if the baby lived through the abortion then he said the baby should be killed.

From the perspective of a former satanist, President Obama sounds like a good friend of Satanists, and the kind of president satan would want in office. Satan wants destruction of innocence. He wants innocent children murdered and he wants there to be no restriction on the killing. And apparently our president feels the same. And now, since his re-election, I wonder how many more babies have been murdered and how much more money he has funneled to Planned Parenthood.

Newborn baby At 40 Weeks

The baby, now approximately seven and a half pounds, is ready for life outside its mother's womb. At birth the placenta will detach from the side of the uterus and the umbilical cord will cease working as the child takes his first breaths of air. The child's breathing will trigger changes in the structure of the heart and bypass arteries which will force all blood to now travel through the lungs.

Has anyone heard of the term "after-birth abortion"? Apparently that is legal and defended quite a bit by Planned Parenthood but late term abortions are allegedly illegal. And the term after birth is as the name implies. Disgusting as it sounds my question is, up to what age can you have this procedure?

If my teenagers are acting out can my wife have a late term after birth abortion? PP argues that these abortions are because this baby will not benefit anyone. This baby will not grow up and be a productive member of society. My dad has COPD & is in a wheelchair and my mom has Lewy Body Dementia that's associated with

Parkinson's Disease, both are in their 80s, according to Planned Parenthood they are no longer (and for quite some time) benefiting society. Is it too late to give them both after birth abortions?

After birth abortion… it sounds so much better than Infanticide, assisted suicide, euthanasia, murder.

Many people like to throw around the bible quote, "Judge not lest ye be judged" but let's look at the quote in its context:

Matthew 7:1-5
"Do not judge so that you will not be judged. For in the way you judge, you will be judged; and by your standard of measure, it will be measured to you. Why do you look at the speck that is in your brother's eye, but do not notice the log that is in your own eye? Or how can you say to your brother, 'Let me take the speck out of your eye,' and behold, the log is in your own eye? You hypocrite, first take the log out of your own eye, and then you will see clearly to take the speck out of your brother's eye."

So many people use this verse as an excuse not to help someone by speaking to them about sin, or as an excuse to not hear what someone has to say particularly about morality. But looking at it in its context changes its misinterpretation and abuse into a clearer picture. This scripture is not admonishing people not to use their God given judgement, but rather about living a Holy life and avoiding hypocrisy and rash judgements. Expecting us to measure ourselves by the rule that we measure others is not a threat, in the Lords Prayer in Matthew 6:12 we ask God to forgive us to the extent that we forgive others. It's an important and Holy way to live our life, in fact we need to be strict with ourselves and more forgiving with others. But Christ is certainly not forbidding us or discouraging us to speak with our brothers who are struggling with sin, or that we shouldn't use a sharpened healthy conscience in judging right and wrong. In fact in multiple places, like 1 Corinthians 5:12-13, and 6:2-18 and Leviticus 19:15 we are told that we SHOULD judge but in righteousness In Matthew 18: 15-17 it says,

"If your brother sins, go and show him his fault in private; if he listens to you, you have won your brother. But if he does not listen to you, take one or two more with you, so that BY THE MOUTH OF TWO OR THREE WITNESSES EVERY FACT MAY BE CONFIRMED. If he refuses to listen to them, tell it to the church; and if he refuses to listen even to the church, let him be to you as a Gentile and a tax collector."

We find most people use "Judge not" as an excuse not to hear hard truths or look in a mirror, or worse… as an excuse to show false love when they are truly afraid of confrontation while they watch someone destroy themselves with sin.

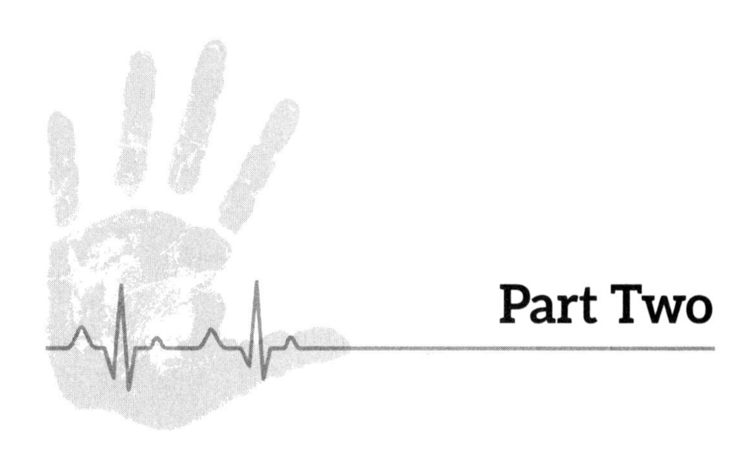

Part Two

Revelations 12:7-12
Fierce war broke out in heaven, where Michael and his angels fought against the dragon. The dragon and his angels fought on their part, but could not win the day, or stand their ground in heaven any longer; the great dragon, serpent of the primal age, was flung down to earth; he whom we call the devil, or Satan, the whole world's seducer, flung down to earth, and his angels with him. Then I heard a voice crying aloud in heaven, The time has come; now we are saved and made strong, our God reigns, and power belongs to Christ, his anointed; the accuser of our brethren is overthrown. Day and night he stood accusing them in God's presence; but because of the Lamb's blood and because of the truth to which they bore witness, they triumphed over him, holding their lives cheap till death overtook them. Rejoice over it, heaven, and all you that dwell in heaven; but woe to you, earth and sea, now that the

devil has come down upon you, full of malice, because he knows how brief is the time given him.

I have two books coming out in the future.

Abortion is a Satanic Sacrifice and Satan Loves Me, He Loves Me Not. Satan loves me he loves me not is an autobiography covering my life within Satanism and the occult from 26 years up to where we are now. That book opens with a story that I'm going to start this section off with as well.

When I was almost 14 I was part of a large satanic coven. A group of males 15 years old and younger had a sleep over at an adult females house. My parents thought I was staying the night at a friends house. The purpose of the sleepover was to impregnate the female for a satanic spell that was to take place approximately 9 months from then. Fast forward 9 months into the future and now I'm about 3 months before turning 15 the entire coven has met for this spell. I'm going to try to paint the most vivid picture I can of that night. I want you to feel like you're watching what I'm saying. You need to understand the gravity of what I'm saying to you. To simply tell you a spell happened or an abortion took place would not do justice to the story.

Abortion is a satanic sacrifice and now I'm going to tell you why I say that.

As I said before, I'm almost 15. It's a Saturday night and all the members of the coven have gathered at one of the members ranch. We are in a large building on the ranch. It has one really large room with a fire place in it with two smaller rooms side by side at one end of the building.

I've been to the building before at a Christmas party when I was 10 or 11 years old. Back when I didn't know what a coven was and I still had some innocence about me.

I've been in this room since about 9pm. We all had snacks about 8pm at the main house. Most people arrived in groups. At 9pm I'm walking around watching what everyone else is doing. Most people are praying or meditating and a few are engaged in sexual activity.

By 10pm everyone has on their ceremonial robes or they have stripped down to what they will be now wearing for the ceremony. At midnight a parchment is read that has the spells intention. Then everyone separates into his or her section. 50 females ranging from about 15 to 60 are kneeling, nude on the floor starting up a chant of 'our bodies, ourselves'. They will continue this chant till the sacrifice at 3am. There is a small group 10-12 kids 3 to 10 years old that are in a room praying to satan for the intention of the group. Really this group is just in training. So they are back at the main house watching movies or cartoons and coloring. But they are wearing costumes of the different robes of black or red and enjoying a party.

Let's take a brief detour here for a moment to mention Baphomet.

After all of the issues in the media regarding the statue of Baphomet, I am sure many of you know what it looks like. But it is an image embraced as a symbol particularly by blatant Satanism but at times Gnosticism in general, it is a goat headed creature with a human torso with breasts and wings, with its arms pointed both above and below it and a pentagram on its forehead, each aspect of its detailed figure is a representation of a different ideology. This is a common perspective of it that Satanists claim to take, these quotes are from famous occultist Eliphas Lévi who came up with the popular drawing or image of this ancient figure "But the adorers of [Baphomet] do not consider...that it is a representation of the devil; on the contrary, for them it is that of the god Pan, the god of our modern schools of philosophy...the god of the primitive Gnostic schools". "Moreover, the sign of occultism is made with both hands, pointing upward to the white moon of Chesed, and downward to the black moon of Geburah. This sign expresses the perfect concord between mercy and justice. One of the arms is feminine and other masculine, as in the Androgyne of Khunrath, whose attributes we have combined with those of our goat, since they are one and the same symbol. The torch of intelligence burning between the horns is the magical light of universal equilibrium; it is also the type of soul exalted above matter, as the flame cleaves to the torch. The monstrous head of the animal expresses horror of sin, for which the material agent, alone responsible, must alone and forever bear the penalty, because the soul is impassible in its nature and can suffer only by materializing. The caduceus, which replaces the generative organ, represents eternal life; the scale-covered belly typifies water; the circle above it is the atmosphere; the feathers still higher up signify the volatile; lastly, humanity is depicted by the two breasts and the androgyny arms of this sphinx of the occult sciences".

Though some more educated Gnostics allege to embrace this image as a symbol of spiritual or philosophical enlightenment, and appreciate each aspect of this creation as representing what their ultimate values are they claim they don't necessarily embrace it as a mockery of God or as a representative of satan. And they will likely throw knowledge of its symbolism and history as a way to claim that you know nothing about the image or their lifestyle or dogma. But most people involved in the occult and Satanism are fully embracing of this image as representative of satan, a powerful occult symbol and a complete mockery of morality, The Holy and ancient symbols of Christianity. It is known that to keep images of Baphomet in their home is to invite the demonic, it is a very specific representation and idol dedicated to various demons, which can assist and grant greater percentage of success in their goals, particularly in occult works.

Thirteen adults are praying in front of a Baphomet and muttering spells under their breath and this activity as well will continue till 3am.

By the way if a child is able to say awake till 3am they will be given a special prize for being able to do so. I have been instructed to walk around and observe all the groups. So from about midnight till about two I sat in with the 13 adults, the kids and the women on the floor.

Then I was instructed to ready myself. This was a big deal for me. These ceremonies happened quite often within our group but this was my first time attending and my first murder, so I was very excited.

At 2am the 13 top coven members stood in a semi circle around the woman that had been impregnated 9 months before. That woman was in a hospital gown, laying on a birthing table with her feet up in stirrups.

The 13 have a quiet spell being chanted over and over. At approximately 2:45 am I'm standing in the semi-circle with a doctor. He asks me if I'm ready and if I've been practicing. I answered yes to both. For the last 2-4 weeks I worked on stabbing a mango, an avocado, a boiled egg and a ball of play-doh with a scalpel.

I did not see what I was doing as killing a baby. But I did recognize that I was taking a life or murdering a person. At least that first time. After that is was explained to me about killing innocents and hurting God.

At 3am I'm dressed in a red robe with my cowl raised. I have on surgical gloves and mask. The doctor is next to me dressed as a doctor. He wasn't just dressed as a doctor though. I personally knew him as a real doctor.

The spell is spoken the final time and an offering is made. I insert the scalpel carefully into the young lady. I've been told to be careful and gentle. We have a sacrifice to make but I am not to hurt the messenger or carrier.

At this point the baby is in the birth canal. I stab carefully a few times into the woman with the scalpel. I still do not know if either the baby or mother had ingested any meds to assist in the abortion or not, and I am not even sure if I was successful in where I was stabbing, I was so nervous at the time.

When I extracted my hand the scalpel and glove were bloody. The doctor then took over. I stood there trembling it was a huge adrenaline rush for me. I had committed my first murder (first of 146 abortions) and it was legal.

The doctor finished up then inserted forceps that looked like scissors with a curved part to go inside the woman and it had jagged teeth.

I stood by the 13 members. We are no longer in a semi-circle now we are facing the women on the floor who are still kneeling, swaying, making a humming or buzzing sound with eyes rolled back in their heads and wild grimaces on their faces as if in a state of demonic ecstasy.

The doctor finishes the procedure then tears the baby apart and throws baby parts out onto the floor in the midst of all the women they immediately pounce on all the parts, fighting for them and devouring them. They cannibalized everything but the bones.

All the females in a possessed blood frenzy start a sex orgy which everyone in the room joins in on.

I'm showered and back in my street clothes by 6am and I've snuck back in my house before 7am. Just in time for my parents to wake up me and my brother and have us get ready and go to church.

I went into a lot of detail on that but I wanted to paint a picture for you. When some people hear I was a Satanist and aborted a baby at 14 I sometimes hear things like 'whoa, cool, how did that feel?' or people that feel sorry for me. Yes the majority feel for the baby but there are too many people that somehow have romanticized what it means to be a Satanist, what a ritual might be like or how an abortion takes place.

I preformed my first abortion when I was 14 years old. Most likely I didn't outright kill the baby. I imagine the doctor did that. But I did assist. That was 1980. Between then and 1985 I assisted in 4 more. All of that was in a coven with about 150 members from a bunch of neighboring towns and counties in the southern part of the United States.

I left that coven when I graduated from high school and started to junior college. Even though that was 60 miles away there were people at school who belonged to my old coven. I joined a fairly large coven at school but all they wanted to do was drink and get high. They did mock spells that they seemed to make up on the spot. Also a lot of the members, although part of a satanic coven, didn't actually worship satan. And some of them went to Christian churches. Not to break them up mind you, but because they viewed their coven as more of a social club. Some place fun to go the night before going to church.

This wasn't what I was looking for. Sure drugs, booze and sex were enjoyable but I could get that anywhere. I thirsted after power and enjoyed, craved and was practically addicted to magick.

I had assisted in a few abortions by then and really craved the power from those events. Being the chief practitioner of magick at these events you have a feeling of being invulnerable or bullet proof. Definitely a feeling of power that lasts for days afterwards. I craved that.

I visited my old coven once in a while and expressed my desires to them. One of their members put me in touch with another coven and I was off and running again.

This coven was also connected to my old coven and shared membership with a few members.

It was at this coven that I learned what a high wizard was and realized this was what I wanted to be. In smaller covens the highest position is a high priest or a high priestess. Sometimes just one and sometimes both. In some larger covens they have multiple high priests and high priestesses. And sometimes there is just one high priest that is shared between covens.

In the World Church of Satan there are 3 types of magick people. There are people that have made it to high priest or priestess and there are multiple ways this happens; to briefly touch on this they can be voted in, self-appointed, chosen, or have somehow overtaken their predecessor.

The second grouping are those that wish to practice magick and hone their skills but do not wish to stop at priest or priestess. Military ranking is how they are categorized. In a smaller coven a high priest may seem like a general. In a large coven the high priest is a sergeant. If they were self-appointed they may be considered a private. Some people aspire to be a high priest or priestess because they incorrectly assume it's the highest position there is. Or it's the top magick position.

The third position is the high wizard there are usually 2 to 5 of these in the world. The number can be as low as one and as many as 10. And they are usually unknown to one another.

I know you are thinking 'how can you belong to the same coven and not know each other'? The world church of satan has at least 6 names. It is a worldwide organization, with membership in almost every country of the world. I actually don't know what countries are not involved, but I know in 1989 there were over 1 million members.

High wizards are generally male but can be female. They also are taken from the rank of lieutenant or higher unless someone sees potential in someone of a lesser rank. And on very, very rare occasions a high priest or priestess gets appointed a high wizard.

You heard correctly they are not voted in, they cannot appoint themselves, they did not kill their predecessor. They were appointed by someone in the upper tiers in the world church of satan. It is said High Wizards are handpicked by satan himself. When you hear of secret societies like the Illuminati, Skull and Bones, Bohemian Grove and the like they all seek high wizards to do their spell work for them.

Before I was made a High Wizard I had been practicing magick for approximately 12 years. To make this clear, this is magick ending with a K & not magic ending in a C. Magic ending in a "C" is generally harmless. Like illusion, the magician at a child birthday party. Someone doing tricks with cards and coins, maybe even a master of illusion, like David Copperfield. Magick with a "K" is what someone does in a coven, as a wiccan or Satanist, the kind of sorcery Harry Potter does and the bible warns against.

I had been a Satanist for 10 years and a member of the World Church of Satan for over 4 years. I had helped split over 20 churches by then and assisted in close to 25 baby murders.

I had done thousands of spells with a 91% success rate. And satan picked me to be a High Wizard.

No one can tell a High Wizard what to do. You can suggest, you can imply and you can request. But the ultimate decision to do the spell or totally ignore the requester is completely up to the High Wizard. Secret Societies, rich, powerful people around the world and politicians all seek the High Wizard.

It was everything I hoped it was. I traveled and worked in the circles of the rich and powerful of the world and helped them mold the planet to what satan wanted it to be. Satan wants complete control over the world. He wants everyone in the world to turn from God. And one of the best ways to do this is population control. Less people are easier to control and people without kids are less likely to fight against some things even if they themselves believe it to be wrong.

But those with children here or on the way will want the world to be a better place for those children.

Satan wants less innocence in and out of the womb and to eliminate the chances of more innocence being created. Think abortion, think sterilization, I'm almost surprised abortion mills and sterilization clinics aren't offering to pay instead of charge for their services.

There are many organizations connected in pushing forward satans agenda. I'm not giving a full history or going into a lot of detail here for a couple of reasons. This CD is about abortion being a satanic sacrifice and how I know this to be true. And every group I talk about here has thousands of pages on the internet about them. There's no way to make one disc comprehensive on any one of them. But just as in any play, movie, or story, it helps if you at least have some character names.

If you are interested in conspiracy theories, or know a few conspiracy theorists you will probably have heard all or most of these names and terms. When dealing with these supposed new world order type conspiracy theories you will find so much truth mixed in with so much insanity it can be near impossible to take it seriously or weed the truth from the paranoia and bizarre thought process.

The information that I am giving you, though the descriptions are summarized and from other sources, are things that I dealt with personally in my life and work. When doing any kind of research into these theories there is one subject that you will not or will rarely see intertwined with all of this… satan and Satanism. Many people who are interested in these subjects aren't discussing them from an angle of spiritual warfare, or the ultimate motivation… they believe it is essentially just money, power, and control that is driving these strange corruptions and manipulations of our world. But the reality is that all of these organizations, and the root of everything is to bring about specific, intentional, satanic agendas. Though most if not all of the people involved are certainly motivated by money, power and control... these are the things satan offers us... the belief that they are somehow getting a better life, more pleasure, and humans are driven by these agendas and a vision of a world where they come out on top, they are being moved by satan and his agendas. Satanism and the occult are the foundation of all of these things, working closely with every one of these groups. Which is essentially what my job was. To involve the occult, while the coven itself worked through these groups to drive these people, with the temptations of material benefits, to satanic goals. Included in this is abortion, as most conspiracy theories will simply include it along with population control, the reality is much more obscene and sinister as abortion is actually about murder, spilling blood, destroying innocence, hurting God, having a mother intentionally kill her own child, and driving humanity to its most disgusting corrupt depths.

Starting off we'll talk about Bohemian Grove

Colossians 3:5
"You must deaden, then, those passions in you which belong to earth, fornication and impurity, lust and evil desire, and that love of money which is an idolatry. These are what bring down God's vengeance on the unbelievers"

To quote an article from the Washington Post by Elizabeth Flock "Every July, some of the richest and most powerful men in the world gather at a 2,700 acre campground in Monte Rio California for two weeks of heavy drinking, super-secret talks, druid worship (the group insists they are simply "revering the Redwoods"), and other rituals.

Their purpose: to escape the "frontier culture", or uncivilized interests, of common men.

The people that gather at Bohemian Grove who have included prominent business leaders, former US presidents, musicians, and oil barons- are told that "weaving spiders come not here" meaning business deals are to be left outside. One exception was in 1942, when a planning for the Manhattan Project took place at the grove, leading to the creation of the atom bomb.

A spokesperson for Bohemian Grove says the people that gather there "Share a passion for the outdoors, music, and theater."

The club is so hush-hush that little can be definitively said about it, but much of what we know today is from those who have infiltrated the camp, including Texas-based filmmaker Alex Jones."

This event is centered around a ceremony called the Cremation of Care. Every July is the burning in effigy of a child sacrifice. They say it's in effigy to so no one knows that they may be sacrificing a real child.

This "sacrifice" happens each year because these politicians and businessmen are engaged in highly unethical practices all year and a sacrifice of innocence to satan gives them their hearts desire or success in their endeavors.

If you watch the video of hidden Bohemian Grove and the Cremation of Care Ceremony footage by filmmaker Alex Jones, available on YouTube, you will see near the end of the video a High Wizard on a boat, dressed in black with his face painted white like a skull.

Bohemian Grove is actually open four times per year. With some of the very rich being allowed to go there whenever they want. It's funny that they give the "no spiders" quote since all they do is business deals. Reporters go and have to sign a non-disclosure so they can't reveal anything they've seen, but now they have access to all the rich and powerful they've ever wanted to interview. Rich and powerful people that you wouldn't think would have any interest in magick or the occult are so steeped in it you can't tell them from hardcore Satanists. People that I'm certain have signed anti-homosexuality bills are engaged in homosexuality. And while abortions don't take place AT the grove they are certainly used in the moving of their agendas. Many of the attendees belong or go to all of the groups listed in this section. The people that go there have done their part to move the abortion agenda forward, and many of these people would be seeking powerful spell work for their objectives to be accomplished, which means occult human sacrifice through abortion. Though ultimately the draw is a combination of rubbing elbows with other people of power and influence, making connections, as well as just unfettered hedonism.

Groups that are all tied together

The Bildebergs
Council on Foreign Relations
World Trade Organization
World Bank Group
Skull and Bones
The Illuminati
Freemasons
OTO
Trilateral Commission

The three things all of these groups have in common is that they are all government related, they are all filled with Satanists, and the end game of all the groups involve population control.

The method I will use to describe each of these topics, is a brief description, most from Wikipedia, and then I will continue with my own comments.

Freemasons

Hebrews 4:12-13
God's word to us is something alive, full of energy; it can penetrate deeper than any two-edged sword, reaching the very division between soul and spirit, between joints and marrow, quick to distinguish every thought and design in our hearts. From him, no creature can be hidden; everything lies bare, everything is brought face to face with him, this God to whom we must give our account.

Regarding the freemasons, we will take a description from Catholic.com: Freemasonry is incompatible with the Catholic faith. Freemasonry teaches a naturalistic religion that espouses indifferentism, the position that a person can be equally pleasing to God while remaining in any religion.

Masonry is a parallel religion to Christianity. The New Catholic Encyclopedia states, "Freemasonry displays all the elements of religion, and as such it becomes a rival to the religion of the Gospel. It includes temples and altars, prayers, a moral code, worship, vestments, feast days, the promise of reward or punishment in the afterlife, a hierarchy, and initiation and burial rites."

Masonry is also a secret society. Its initiates subscribe to secret blood oaths that are contrary to Christian morals. The prospective Mason swears that if he ever reveals the secrets of Masonry - secrets which are trivial and already well-known - he wills to be subject to self-mutilation or to gruesome execution. (Most Masons, admittedly, never would dream of carrying out these punishments on themselves or on an errant member).

Historically, one of Masonry's primary objectives has been the destruction of the Catholic Church; this is especially true of Freemasonry as it has existed in certain European countries. In the United States, Freemasonry is often little more than a social club, but it still espouses a naturalistic religion that contradicts orthodox Christianity. (Those interested in joining a men's club should consider the Knights of Columbus instead.)

The Church has imposed the penalty of excommunication on Catholics who become Freemasons.

Freemasons are one of the most evil organizations in the world. They are so nefarious, if your friends played a joke on you and drugged you, and brought you to a freemason meeting, not a low level temple, but a higher one, and that's where you woke up, you'd think you just woke up in the scariest satanic coven meeting you've ever come to... not realizing that it's your run of the mill ho hum high level freemason temple. These guys openly worship the devil, they do mock sacrifices that look real. They wear scary costumes, satanic robes, and they openly fight the church. Lower level freemasons swear allegiance to Jesus, not realizing that if they don't go up any higher, they'll never know how bad their group is. At a lot of the events that I've been to, that I describe here, freemasons provide security. Like for Bohemian grove, they provide the security for where the cooks and bus people park their cars, and from the main parking lot. They generally don't come into the grove itself but they recognize the grove as just a bunch of 'boys being boys' and partying up, and they know they like to do that. As a side note, I occasionally work with exorcists around the world. And many times when we're trying to discover the root cause of someones possession, it will be revealed that a past family member was a 33rd degree freemason. When the mason becomes a 33rd degree, they curse everybody in their family from them forward. From early on oaths were made for many things nonsensical, with the threat of death if you broke it, then you would be made to break the oath, and nothing would happen as punishment so by slowing wearing down the value of an oath by the time the person is making luciferian oaths, and cursing their family, they don't take it for what it truly is.

World Bank

Matthew 16:26
"How is a man the better for it, if he gains the whole world at the cost of losing his own soul? For a man's soul, what price can be high enough?"

World Bank is an international financial institution that provides loans to developing countries for capital programs. It comprises two institutions: the International Bank for Reconstruction and Development (IBRD) and the International Development Association (IDA). The World Bank is a component of the World Bank Group, and a member of the United Nations Development Group.

The World Bank's official goal is the reduction of poverty.

In case any of you have forgotten, Margret Sanger said, years and years ago, that we can reduce poverty by killing our babies before they're born. This thought was not lost on these companies listed herein. That is the satanic agenda rhetoric they constantly spout. We can eliminate poverty, world hunger, pollution and over population (which nowhere really has) by aborting babies. I would almost be willing to bet that if the world stopped aborting babies all of the world's problems would pan out. We would finally make God happy in something and no one can out charity God.

World Trade Organization

Luke 12: 15-21
"Then he said to them, "Look well and keep yourselves clear of all covetousness. A man's life does not consist in having more possessions than he needs. And he told them a parable, "There was a rich man whose lands yielded a heavy crop: and he debated in his mind, 'What am I to do, with no room to store my crops in?' Then he said, 'This is what I will do; I will pull down my barns, and build greater ones, and there I shall be able to store all my harvest and all the goods that are mine; and then I will say to my soul, Come, soul, thou hast goods in plenty laid up for many years to come; take thy rest now, eat, drink, and make merry.' And God said, 'Thou fool, this night thou must render up thy soul; and who will be master now of all thou hast laid by?' Thus it is with the man who lays up treasure for himself, and has no credit with God."

The World Trade Organization is an intergovernmental organization which regulates international trade. The WTO deals with regulation of trade between participating countries by providing a framework for negotiating trade agreements and a dispute resolution process aimed at enforcing participants' adherence to WTO agreements, which are signed by representatives of member governments and ratified by their parliaments.

Not only do Satanists attend these meetings, the WTO is comprised of a bunch of Satanists. Satan knows the best way to infiltrate is from the inside, the best way to get what he wants is to take over every organization that somehow touches something that he wants. On the outside the WTO's agreements may look wonderful, they may look 'win-win' obviously with every set of agreements there are compromises to be made, oddly enough a lot of their agreements and their compromises deal in dead babies.

Council on Foreign Relations

Luke 6:43-49
"There is no sound tree that will yield withered fruit, no withered tree that will yield sound fruit. Each tree is known by its proper fruit; figs are not plucked from thorns, nor grapes gathered from brier bushes. A good man utters what is good from his heart's store of goodness; the wicked man, from his heart's store of wickedness, can utter nothing but what is evil; it is from the heart's overflow that the mouth speaks."

The Council on Foreign Relations (CFR), founded in 1921, is a United States nonprofit, 4900 member organization, publisher, and think tank specializing in U.S. foreign policy and international affairs, headquartered in New York City, with an additional office in

Washington, D.C. Its membership has included senior politicians, more than a dozen secretaries of state, CIA directors, bankers, lawyers, professors, and senior media figures.

You cannot discuss all the worlds nefarious organizations without mentioning them. The CFR works hand in hand with all the major players, they are smack dab in the middle of helping all the countries in the world that can't help themselves. Eliminate their poverty etc etc etc. And I know it's beginning to sound like a broken record, and I'm tired to saying it, why does every one of these so called solutions end in dead babies? Keep in mind again that many of the people involved in these organizations are NOT looking at it from the perspective of putting an end to human suffering… they are working in conjunction with satanic organizations to complete a goal. While many well meaning people may actually feel that population control is a genuine solution to problems in our world, it is a mentality that has been shoved in our face for so many years that it's more about what incredible manipulators these people are to convince such a number of our population into truly believing that human life does not hold enough value to be nurtured and supported, and that it's better we were killed off at our most vulnerable all in the name of mercy. To quote Mother Theresa, "It is a poverty to decide that a child must die so that you may live as you wish."

The Bilderberg Group

Matthew 15: 10 & 11
"Then he gathered the multitude about him, and said to them, "Listen to this, and grasp what it means. It is not what goes into a man's mouth that makes him unclean; what makes a man unclean is what comes out of his mouth."

The Bilderberg Group, Bilderberg Conference or Bilderberg Club is an annual private conference of approximately 120 to 140 invited guests from North America and Europe, most of whom are people of influence. About one-third are from government and politics, and two-thirds from finance, industry, labor, education and communications. The Original conference was held in hotel de Bilderberg in 1945 in the Netherlands.

Historically, attendee lists have been weighted towards bankers, politicians, and directors of large businesses. Including heads of state and prominent politicians from North America and Europe.

One of the groups primary goals is a one world government which fits the New World Order.

The Bilderberg Group can actually be divided into two sections, the core group that has an agenda, and wants to move their agenda forward. And the attendees who are invited that they need to help to move their agenda forward. The Core is generally 12-30 members, and they don't change. The rest of the group changes according to need.

People that are members of the Bilderberg Group are often times members of some of the other nefarious groups listed here. Like some members of the Trilateral Commission and the CFR are the same people. People that belong to the Bilderberg Group are also in the Illuminati. They also go to Bohemian Grove, they're also Freemasons. Some of them would also be Bones Men. They are huge fans of the World Church of Satan, and Satanists have a standing invitation at all Bilderberg meetings. Although a one world order is their ultimate goal one of their major functions is that they organize the different abortion providers all around the world, they connect them with the right group that is willing to pay for them to set up different facilities around the world.

Unfortunately, my job as a high wizard for 12 years had me working with groups that are for lack of a better term, conspiracy related, and usually when someone is speaking on these topics they tend to get lumped in as "a conspiracy theorist nut-job".

The reason that I am bringing up these issues in relation to government organizations and my experiences with them, is because I want to share that beyond my own involvement in actively using abortion in the occult, it is not just an issue with individual clinics, it is a problem worldwide. It is not a small lump of wacko occultists supporting the abortion movement, it is ingrained and it is very intentional. And while it is very important to march, to protest, to show people that killing other humans is unacceptable on the ground level… the most influence we can have on this issue as Christians, is through spiritual warfare.

The Trilateral Commission

Mark 7:18-23
"And he said to them, Are you still so slow of wit? Do you not observe that all the uncleanness which goes into a man has no means of defiling him, because it travels, not into his heart, but into the belly, and so finds its way into the sewer? Thus he declared all meat to be clean, and told them that what defiles a man is that which comes out of him. For it is from within, from the hearts of men, that their wicked designs come, their sins of adultery, fornication, murder, theft, covetousness, malice, deceit, lasciviousness, envy, blasphemy, pride and folly. All these evils come from within, and it is these which make a man unclean."

The Trilateral Commission is another organization like the Bildeberg council on foreign relations and others. It is a shadow company that has aligned itself with Freemasons and the Illuminati to help form a one world government.

The following portion on the Trilateral Commission is from a fairly comprehensive article featured on Canadafreepress.com.

"The Trilateral Commission is international and is intended to be the vehicle for multinational consolidation of the commercial and banking interests by seizing control of the political government of the U.S." - Sen. Barry Goldwater.

When looking at the facts on the Trilateral Commission, it's important to understand that it was set up as a front for the exact same goals of the Council on Foreign Relations.

The Trilateral Commission is another tool used by the leaders of the CFR shadow government.

The world's elite utilizes secretive organizations such as the Committee of 300 structure, the CFR, the Bilderberg Society, and the Trilateral Commission to further its ultimate goal of global domination.

Although all these groups play a part in the movement toward a One World Government, the facts on the Trilateral Commission all lead us more specifically to the Council on Foreign Relations.

The Trilateral commission and the CFR work hand in hand with each other, Satanism, the Illuminati. However they don't like High Wizards… because they wear costumes, and looks like a rock star or a clown in their opinion, and they prefer to work as professional conservative business persons. They were much happier if they could find someone who would wear a suit and blend in. It was difficult to work in a situation where every one of us had huge egos and wanted the upper hand.

As with most of these organizations, one of their primary objectives is to encourage wealthy countries to be philanthropic and support poor countries by providing abortions and sterilizations.

Skull and Bones

1 Timothy 6:7-12
"Empty-handed we came into the world, and empty-handed, beyond question, we must leave it; why then, if we have food and clothing to last us out, let us be content with that. Those who would be rich fall into temptation, the devil's trap for them; all those useless and dangerous appetites which sink men into ruin here and perdition hereafter. The love of money is a root from which every kind of evil springs, and there are those who have wandered away from the faith by making it their ambition, involving themselves in a world of sorrows."

Skull and Bones is an undergraduate senior secret society at Yale University, New Haven, Connecticut. It is the oldest senior class landed society at Yale. The society's alumni organization the Russel Trust Association, owns the society's real estate and oversees the organization. The society is known informally as "Bones" and members are known as "Bonesmen".

This society is infamous for several of its members gaining positions of power and wealth... such as president Taft, both President Bushes, Senator John F Kerry and many others including Henry Luce nicknamed "Baal" who was the founder and publisher of Time magazine.

I include the Skull and Bone society, because I personally knew of some of the occult and nefarious activities that happened in this place. There's a one world agenda and the bonesmen play a role in that. It is a way to groom the offspring of the rich and powerful to push this agenda, and be more easily used in their plans. Skull and bones incorporates Freemasonry, The Illuminati, and witchcraft, oft times black magick ceremonies in with their own occult activities. And in essence, water down what they are doing to just be fun and games, sort of like the Freemasons watering down what an oath means so that by the time they are doing lucifarian oaths they mean nothing, at least to the unwitting member.

The Illuminati

Luke 12:2 & 3
"What is veiled will all be revealed, what is hidden will all be known; what you have said in darkness, will be repeated in the light of day, what you have whispered in secret chambers, will be proclaimed on the house-tops."

The Illuminati is made up of the worlds political and financial elite. They are in charge of assassinations, currency control, population control, world governments, world entertainment etc. Some believe the Illuminati started in Bavaria, some believe they started in France. I know they have a library and museum in France but have no idea where they really started.

Reading a description from Wikipedia: The Illuminati is a name given to several groups, both real and fictitious. Historically the name refers to the Bavarian Illuminati, an Enlightenment-era secret society founded on May 1, 1776 to oppose superstition, prejudice, religious influence over public life, abuses of state power and to support women's education and gender equality. The illuminati were outlawed along with other secret societies by the Bavarian government leadership with the encouragement of the Roman Catholic Church, and permanently disbanded in 1785. In the several years following, the group was vilified by conservative and religious critics who claimed they had regrouped and were responsible for the French Revolution.

In subsequent use, the "Illuminati" refers to various organizations claiming or purported to have unsubstantiated links to the original Bavarian Illuminati or similar secret societies, and often alleged to conspire to control world affairs by masterminding events and planting agents in government and corporations to establish a New World Order and gain further political power and influence. Central to some of the most widely known and elaborate conspiracy theories, the Illuminati have been depicted as lurking in the shadows and pulling the strings and levers of power in dozens of novels, movies, television shows, comics, video games, and music videos. ... The organization seems to have been modeled on the Freemasons and it drew membership from existing Masonic lodges.

Some people believe the Illuminati is anti-Catholic which makes the most sense since Catholics are anti-evil and the Illuminati is run by Satanists. However, conspiracy theorists also like to assume the pope is a member of the Illuminati which on some levels makes sense since it seems almost all world leaders are members or connected somehow.

Having worked within organized Satanism for 20+ years and having worked closely with the Illuminati for approximately 12 of those years I can say that I never met the pope or anyone higher than a Catholic priest.

The Catholic Priest was a not a member of the Illuminati, it was just someone I met while I was a Satanist, who was a Satanist as well, infiltrating the church.

OTO

Matthew 24:42-51
"You must be on the watch, then, since you do not know the hour of your Lord's coming. Be sure of this; if the master of the house had known at what time of night the thief was coming, he would have kept watch, and not allowed his house to be broken open. And you too must stand ready; the Son of Man will come at an hour when you are not expecting him. Which of you, then, is a faithful and wise servant, one whom his master will entrust with the care of the household, to give them their food at the appointed time? Blessed is that servant who is found doing this when his lord comes; I promise you, he will give him charge of all his goods. But if that servant plays him false, and says in his heart, My lord is long in coming, and so falls to beating his fellow servants, to eating and drinking with the drunkards, then on some day when he expects nothing, at an hour when he is all unaware, his lord will come, and will cut him off, and assign him his portion with the hypocrites; where there will be weeping, and gnashing of teeth."

Ordo Templi Orientis (O.T.O.) ('Order of the Temple of the East' or 'Order of Oriental Templars') is an international fraternal and religious organization founded at the beginning of the 20th century. English author and occultist Aleister Crowley has become the best-known member of the order.

Originally it was intended to be modelled after and associated with European Freemasonry, such as Masonic Templar organizations, but under the leadership of Aleister Crowley, O.T.O. was reorganized around the Law of Thelema as its central religious principle. This Law—expressed as "Do what thou wilt shall be the whole of the Law" and "Love is the law, love under will"—was promulgated in 1904 with the writing of The Book of the Law.

Keep in mind as well that Aleister Crowley at the time was nicknamed the 'Wickedest man in the world" he was self-proclaimed "666 the beast". One of the most common supposed "facts" that my cult spoke about Crowley was that he had raped and killed a young boy, and was kicked out of a country for it. Since then it seems impossible to find any proof or information on this supposed occurrence, but 30 years ago it was the most common subject spoken about him in the circles I was in, and it certainly wasn't farfetched.

He wrote several books on magick, and he originated the spelling of magick with a K in reference to the occult to distinguish it from illusion or sleight of hand. He also wrote 18 books of poetry.

The first coven I belonged to, the one that taught me that it was okay to kill a baby as long as it was still inside the mother, the organization that had me do my first five abortions, got me involved in child pornography when I was 12, and introduced me to a world of evil, was a branch of the OTO. It had two names that it went by, T'OTO or TOTO, the extra 'T' was for The OTO, the other name was Diablo Sex. Any coven that embraces the name 'diablo sex' is involved in child prostitution, child pornography, and human trafficking.

As I've said in the past, the World Church of Satan is extremely popular within all the nefarious groups in section two. But we weren't the only cult. Now I know a lot of people when you think of a satanic coven you think of some 15 year old pimply faced boy out in the cemetery playing with a Ouija board with his girlfriend. My old coven as of 1989 had 1.1 million members world wide. The OTO likewise is very large and has a lot of affiliates. My first coven was one of its affiliates and it had at any given time 120-150 members. There are as well other satanic covens, satan has quite a web of deceit spun. My second coven is the only one that uses high wizards as far as I know but the OTO has their magick people as do other satanic covens. One of the OTO's main goals other than world wide domination and population control, are mind control and owning their own country, and they believe that these people that they are in league with politically will help attain that goal.

They were essentially my competition in Satanism as one of the largest satanic organizations in the world, since people would generally either pay for our services, or would go to the OTO.

If you've never heard of these groups but would like to do more research into them it can be pretty tricky. There is a lot of information out there, and a lot of truth, but often even more untruth and it can be difficult to maneuver. One of the recommendations that I have when looking for a site with reliable information on these topics is that you avoid any website that attacks the Catholic church… while there are certainly problems with infiltrations and corruptions… many of these sites will make claims like "the pope is a freemason" or "every pope has been a member of the illuminati" and then they will show freeze framed photos of popes holding up the "I love you" sign language gesture and claim it means the pope worships satan. No matter how genuine their information seems to be, if they are so wrong as to lump The Catholic church in with these groups, it would be hard to trust anything else they may say.

It's tough to look at an unborn baby completely mutilated. If people aren't recognizing the fetus or lump of tissue as being a human being why is it so offensive?

Why do people complain when they see pictures or posters of the legal results of baby murder if they truly don't see the fetus as a baby. A lump of cells is just that. A lump of cells. Maybe it's offensive because their subconscious recognizes what they're seeing as a baby. Why do you think they don't see it that way?

Satans lying through his teeth and these people have bought into the lie and here we are.

There are Christians that will say I need to show more love and compassion to those that are getting abortions. I'm not attacking the average person getting an abortion. I'm attacking satan for making and keeping it legal. And Satanists for committing abortions and dedicating them all to satan. I absolutely have sympathy for the ones who have murdered their own children, whether they understood what they were doing or not. They need to go to confession. They need to not be in mortal sin. They need forgiveness and they need to be healed.

I helped murder 146 babies that never got to worship God, love their mother, cure cancer, have their own babies or experience the good and bad that life has to offer. And they all died nameless.

You keep hearing me spout off 146 but it's just a number. So I thought I would name them. God knows what their real names are. But by naming them, all of them, it puts in perspective how many 146 really is.

I picked many of these names from people that I know, this makes it even more personal for me. Now I'm naming people that I'm close to, my life would be empty if any of these people were absent from it, every one of these children are people missing from our world.

Zac
Katie
John
Ann
Johnny
Christina
Chris
Anthony
Jerry
Barbara
Carrie Ann
Joshua
Brian
Eric
Thomas
Julie
Melissa
Fred
Nigel
Ann
David
Johnny
Aaron
Scott
Daniel

Laura
Dennis
Donna
Hunter
Dalton
Dillan
Herbert
Zacharia
Johnathan
Nathan
Lynn
Ronald
Steve
Lisa
Myrta
Richard
Edwin
Donald
Harry
Lauren
William
Allen
Alexander
Danielle
Perry

Amy
Angela
Ardys
Arthur
Barbie
Becky
Bill
Bob
Murphy
Bonny
Brad
Cabbot
Marco
Cass
Charles
Corin
John
Crystal
Brook
Caitlin
Shawna
Christian
Daemon
Nicole
Dana

Diego
Brandon
Cannon
Carrie
Sean
Chip
Brenda
Cynthia
Darryl
Brandy
Carrol
Cathleene
Chris
Chrys
Dameon
Eav
Kaya
Elizabeth
Ethan
Rose
Frank
Brett
Caroline
Chelsea
Claude
Debra
Burke
Chad
Curtis
Charlie
Clare
Cori
Darren
Devon
Efua
Dawn
Courtney
Craig
Dave
Drew
Hannah
Elliot
Finn
Kelly
Gabby
Gary
Glenda
Garth
Erin
Dwight
Emily
Gail
Georgie
Greg
Heather
Ignatius
Jamal
Joleine
Kareem
Kidada
Leena
Jason
Lewis
Jessica
Marcia
Mehmet
Miles
Jole
Wayne
Jesus
& Anne Marie

We lift these names up to the Lord and pray for them. God knows their real names.

Satanism is all about blood sacrifices.

God made blood a binding agent in agreements, contracts and covenants. Satan uses blood in the same manner to make it binding, he also adds in freewill. For example, a cutter will cut their body somewhere, using their freewill. Once blood appears, if there weren't demons present before the cutting started, now they are attracted to the cutter. You now have a blood contract through a demon and therefore through satan because you have exercised your freewill and offered a blood sacrifice, yourself.

You are past the point of temptation you are teetering between oppression and obsession and heading towards possession. Now let's change this up just a bit. NOW let's imagine the young woman who uses her freewill to murder something living inside herself. That seems like a pretty significant blood sacrifice. Free will, blood sacrifice and demonic entities are attracted to death and destruction. It's probably a safe bet that demons reside at abortion clinics.

How could they not with all the freewill sacrifices going on?

Some people ask why we include such horrific descriptions in our CD or will include horrific images in our DVD. Any website you visit to see the results of anything, if you can't see the results it's too hard to make a decision. When I was researching what kind of a car to buy if none of the websites had pictures I still might not have a car. The same goes for researching anything; plane crashes, cancer, clothes, beautiful vacation spots, and yes, abortion.

Satan has convinced people of much. New age religions flourish. A religion is new age if one of these four elements is missing: God, Satan, Heaven, or Hell. A religion doesn't have to worship satan to be satanic. All you have to do is not worship God, The Father.

A lot of people don't get it. Satan, is an ego maniac, he would love it if everyone worshipped him. But ultimately, he wants everyone to not worship God. So, if he can invent thousands of religions to confuse and confound and take not only God out of the picture but himself as well it looks like he's got you.

Satan has convinced many that he's not real. There a line from one of my favorite movies "The Usual Suspects" where the character Verbal Kent quotes Charles Baudelaire saying "The greatest trick the devil ever pulled was convincing the world he doesn't exist."

He'd like you to believe that God isn't real. The bible isn't real. The shroud of Turin is fake. By the way as a side note here on the shroud ChurchMilitant.tv has the results of a five year study where it was learned that the image of Christ that is burned onto the shroud was done so with a blast of 3400 billion watts of VUV radiation. And just in case you're wondering why we don't just duplicate the procedure... it's because we can't. The strongest VUV lights currently offer only a few billion watts of radiation.

There are a lot of things satan has convinced many of. There are some within the abortion community that know abortion is a satanic sacrifice. But the majority of people getting abortions have no clue. Because satan lies and doesn't want you to know the truth. If you knew God was real and heaven was a real place you could go and if you continued your ungodly behavior hell was in your future wouldn't you change?

Satan knows you would and thus he's not going to tell you the truth. People will fight you on this issue tooth and nail. They will call you old fashioned. Scream and yell at you. Get angry and possibly even physically attack you. Some of these people have had abortions. They have been part of a blood sacrifice, and now they are influenced by demons. And demons know how to be clever, deceptive and violent. And are very seldom gentle.

Remember too, most of these people are victims. They are missing a part of themselves. Those that have had abortions are missing their children. Those that abort their children are not avoiding motherhood, they are now mothers to dead children.

Regardless of whether they've had an abortion or not, if they are in favor of abortion, for any reason, they have been lied to about it from someone. Even the best intentioned person who thinks their answer through and thought they got the answer from a great source… if the answer was "Get an abortion", satan, the master of lies and deception, has infiltrated.

We've been trying to do this disc for almost three years. And three years ago I was going to bring up a plethora of hypothetical situations. One of those hypotheticals was, what if you heard Planned Parenthood sold body parts and or organs of dead babies? However since as the follys of man have it, we are three years late putting out our CD, it is November 2015, and the world has now seen 8 videos of Planned Parenthood admitting to selling baby body parts. So that's no longer a hypothetical situation. What's kind of hard for me to grasp is how upset people are that they're selling body parts. It seems to me that the truly upsetting part of that is that they have to murder the baby to get the organ… why aren't we more upset about the blatant killing of over 57 million babies? But since it's these hypothetical… oh wait… that one's not hypothetical anymore… situations that are getting people so upset, please allow me to reveal a few other hypothetical situations…

Now… as I said… These are hypothetical… I obviously have no proof and I'm just saying really… not that abortion clinics have done this, but what if you found out they've done this, would this be upsetting to you? There's an organization and or cult that eat dead babies. They bake them into breads, make them into stews and soups, and their members digest them. How do you think they get these body parts and these babies? They don't kill them themselves. They go out and buy them. Whole sale, in bulk. Where do you suppose you're able to buy dead babies in bulk? There's a doll maker that puts a plastic synthesized skin over a whole dead baby, the people that buy these dolls KNOW what's underneath that skin. I understand it's not a cheap process. I also understand it's cheap for him to buy the babies. Once again, where do you think he gets those babies from? And this last one is the most nefarious hypothetical to me, aside from, for them to get this baby for this purpose, someone had to kill it first. There's a diablo sex organization that is involved in pedophile necrophilia. And if this video could be found, it would shock and disgust the world. I don't think I have to go into detail on this one. But I would like to reiterate the question... where are they getting the babies from? One other thing I'd like to bring up, earlier this year, the Lepanto institute did an interview of me that came out in August 2015, and I think at that time we had 7 or 8 Planned Parenthood secret videos out. And I was accused of trying to ride the coat tails of those videos. Did you know that what's revealed in those videos was revealed by Mark Crutcher with Life Dynamics around 1993? But back then, we didn't have the social media that we have now. So it basically remained a secret until this year. I as well came out with my story in January

2008, and it hasn't changed. So perhaps the videos are riding on Life Dynamics coat tails.

I would like to share with you two quotes from Mother Theresa:

> "We must not be surprised when we hear of murders, of killings, of wars, of hatred. If a mother can kill her own child, what is left but for us to kill each other."
>
> The greatest destroyer of love and peace is abortion, which is war against the child. The mother doesn't learn to love, but kills to solve her own problems. Any country that accepts abortion is not teaching its people to love, but to use any violence to get what they want."

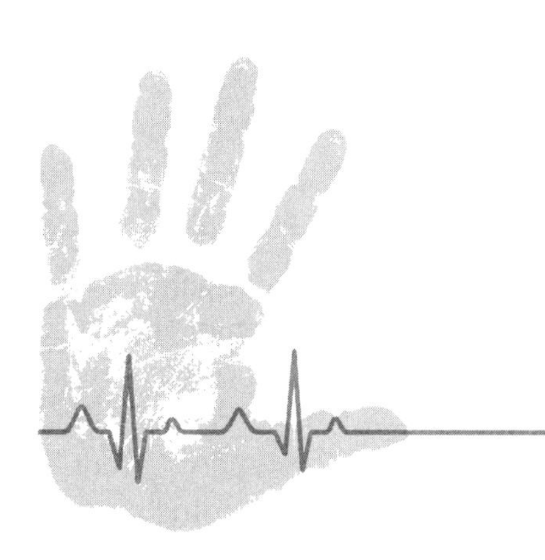

Part Three

Ephesians 6:12-18

It is not against flesh and blood that we enter the lists; we have to do with princedoms and powers, with those who have mastery of the world in these dark days, with malign influences in an order higher than ours. Take up all God's armour, then; so you will be able to stand your ground when the evil time comes, and be found still on your feet, when all the task is over. Stand fast, your loins girt with truth, the breastplate of justice fitted on, and your feet shod in readiness to publish the gospel of peace. With all this, take up the shield of faith, with which you will be able to quench all the fire-tipped arrows of your wicked enemy; make the helmet of salvation your own, and the sword of the spirit, God's word. Use every kind of prayer and supplication; pray at all times in the spirit; keep awake to that end with all perseverance; offer your supplication for all the saints.

I would like to start this section of Abortion is a Satanic Sacrifice by stating right out in the open, that Abortion is spiritual warfare. I do not believe that there is a law that we will write, or a mandate, or a directive, or a statute that will suddenly bring abortion to a halt. If that were the case we DIDN'T have abortion for 200 years, we would have stopped it before it started, yet now that the juggernaut is going, everything we do to try and stop it appears to do nothing. As well, we send over 600,000 people to march in Washington, each year that number gets bigger and bigger. Now currently there's a media blackout every year in Washington during that time. The only media that shows up is just about EWTN and Michael Voris. But mainstream press takes a holiday during that time. If we decided to all stay home, that's when the media blackout would be lifted. And all the major networks would show up. So we have to maintain a major presence just on the off chance that major networks show up one day to see what's happening in Washington. But I do not believe we can send enough people for abortion mills to just shut down one day. I believe that if all 7 billion people in the world showed up, the following day would be business as usual at every abortion mill. In January 2014 the pro-life side sent 630,000 people to march. I was curious as to how many people showed up on the Pro Death side. It took me a long time to find that information. I found information on three sites…

one of them said 30 people, that's not 30,000 people, just 30. Another website said 100, and the third website said 1000. Just for the sake of argument let's say there was 1000. Does anybody remember all the stories in the Old Testament about God's chosen people and their enemies? Do you remember the story of 630,000 good guys getting defeated by 1,000 bad? I can remember the opposite, 1000 good beating a huge number of bad… on what planet could 1000 satanists defeat 630,000 God fearing people? Well, apparently Earth. Because 630,000 of us marched. And almost 2 years later abortion is still legal. Anybody want to venture a guess why? Because satan knows that it's spiritual warfare, and our side hasn't caught up yet. Satan knows he doesn't have to send anybody, why not? Because it's spiritual warfare. If it wasn't spiritual warfare, we would have won by now. But since its spiritual warfare, and we're not fighting the correct way, we're losing. Prayerfully, this CD set will help turn things around.

An acquaintance of mine gave a great analogy... that spiritual warfare, is like a chess match… but the Protestants are playing without their Queen or Bishops.

In regards to spiritual warfare, the Catholic Church is unparalleled.

Our faithful passionate Protestant brothers and sisters are not weaponless by any means… they are able to announce Christ as our Savior, they are able to pray with fervor, and most Protestant faiths do have a valid Baptism.

However... nearly all Protestant religions believe in Sola Scriptura... or that we must only accept the bible alone, as a source of understanding our faith.

They don't recognize Tradition, or a living faith, or the great scholars, theologians and philosophers from the very earliest documents describing the first Christian churches, written and handed down by the very people that studied with the Apostles themselves. They don't recognize the people that studied, lived, and died for the teachings of Christ, handing down the teachings of Christ and His Apostles to all of us, inspired by the Holy Spirit and gifted with incredible reasoning and intellect, devoting their entire lives to understanding the teachings held in the bible. Many don't even realize that there was a living Church for hundreds of years before the bible as we know it was even compiled, and that the Church Herself, through the Holy Spirit, brought the Holy Scriptures together as proof of Her teachings and Dogma.

This means that along with a very inconsistent belief system, a great many of the most vital aspects of spiritual warfare are missing from their arsenal. Including but not limited to:

Apostolic succession, and priestly authority over the demonic.

True exorcism.

Sacramentals, such as holy water, oil and salt, blessed candles and incense.
The sacraments, particularly The Eucharist and an understanding of mortal sin and confession.
Deliverance ministry.
The use of powerful prayer traditions such as Novenas, Chaplets, The Chotki and The Rosary.
and
The role of our Blessed Mother, and the saints in assisting us.

A little later in this disc I will go into more detail on my conversion story. But for now...

When I was confronted with the Blessed Mother at my conversion, after I had accepted Jesus and the Catholic Church, she told me my job was to help end abortion. Ever since January 2008, which was when my conversion happened, I have been telling people the ways to end abortion. Everyone smiles and nods when they hear, but it seems like no-one follows through. The Blessed Mother hasn't changed her tune, she on occasion still tells me this is my job. This is why you're all getting this set. When I tell lay people they smile and nod, and when I tell priests they tell me they would need the bishops permission. I feel like it's a polite way to tell me 'no'. I'm going to present you with the ways I know to shut down an abortion clinic.

Prayerfully, you listening to this disc will follow through.

Matthew 17:14-20
When they reached the multitude, a man came up and knelt before him: Lord, he said, have pity on my son, who is a lunatic, and in great affliction; he will often throw himself into the fire, and often into water. I brought him here to thy disciples, but they have not been able to cure him. Jesus answered, Ah, faithless and misguided generation, how long must I be with you, how long must I bear with you? Bring him here before me. And Jesus checked him with a word, and the devil came out of him; and from that hour the boy was cured. Afterwards, when they were alone, the disciples came to Jesus and asked, 'Why was it that we could not cast it out?' Jesus said to them, 'Because you had no faith. I promise you, if you have faith, though it be but like a grain of mustard seed, you have only to say to this mountain, Remove from this place to that, and it will remove; nothing will be impossible to you. But there is no way of casting out such spirits as this except by prayer and fasting.'

When explaining a way to shut down an abortion mill, remember that these mills are filled with demons, and many of the people that work there have demonic attachment or are entirely possessed. When you're dealing with something like blood sacrifice it essentially consecrates that property to satan, and it is protected in many ways by the demons that inhabit that space. Think of it as a sort of satanic bubble. And if you can pop that so called bubble, and reclaim that ground, that will make it much easier to spiritually attack the evil happening there and reach the people involved.

At Matthew 10:16 Jesus says "Remember, I am sending you out to be like sheep among wolves; you must be wary, then, as serpents, and yet innocent as doves."

A lot of people wonder how long of a fast would be needed for something like this. Three days came to me in Adoration. It doesn't have to be one person fasting for three days, it can be multiple people taking shifts over a 72 hour period, and even then possibly not a full 72 hour period, as in Jesus's death and resurrection took place over 3 days but not 72 hours. Keep in mind by me saying, three days, or by me saying fasting, that just means that you're doing without something, not necessarily food, for three days. With no guarantee of anything in return.

In 2004 a group of pro-life activists started a tradition of fasting and prayer outside of an abortion clinic in Bryan Texas over the course of 40 days. By 2007 it was a nationwide movement and now it is around the world involving hundreds of thousands of people.

As of 2013, that first abortion mill in Bryan Texas, shut down.

Remember, I am sending you out to be like sheep among wolves; you must be wary, then, as serpents, and yet innocent as doves.

No spiritual warfare event would be complete without an exorcism. Most priests are able to do an exorcism of a building or property, they generally don't need to be an actual exorcist, although that might help. And I don't believe that they need the bishops' permission to do this. But, it is important to remember that apostolic succession is very important in spiritual warfare and under no circumstances should this be attempted by a lay person or a non-Catholic priest. That could actually make the situation worse.

Reading from Catholicculture.org February 20, 2012.

For decades, local Catholics had maintained a prayerful presence outside an abortion clinic in Rockford, Illinois, but the clinic remained open.

According to Kevin Rilott of the Rockford Pro-Life Initiative, the tide began to turn in 2009 when Bishop Thomas Doran granted priests permission to recite prayers of exorcism outside the Northern Illinois Women's Center. At times, four priests would stand outside the four corners of the building and recite the prayers together.

"Within two to three weeks of priests saying these prayers, the number of abortions began to drop," said

Rilott. "Over a few months, the number of abortions was cut in half and the numbers of women seeking our help probably doubled. The clinic, which had been performing 25-75 abortions a week for years, also reduced its days of business from three to two." In late 2011, the State of Illinois temporarily suspended the clinic's license; in January, the clinic announced that it would not reopen its doors.

Remember, I am sending you out to be like sheep among wolves; you must be wary, then, as serpents, and yet innocent as doves.

Wouldn't it be great if while we're all out fighting to close down the abortion clinic, if Jesus showed up to help us. That seems like it would be a real smack down. Well there's one of the awesome things about being Catholic. Request that a priest bring a monstrance and do a Eucharistic procession around the building or around the block, When doing that, I would also recommend someone carrying the picture of Our Lady of Guadalupe, it is one of the most powerful devotions we have as Catholics... the Blessed mother is pregnant with Jesus in this picture. It is incredibly powerful, it converted 9 million pagan Aztecs to Christianity within 7 years. As well as the people in the procession should be praying a rosary. I also want to bring up here that another group that recognizes the power of the Eucharist are Satanist. Many satanic cults recognize the True Presence of Christ in the Eucharist, which is why the consecrated Hosts are stolen and desecrated in their ceremonies.

A pro-life group in central Florida was able to shut down two abortion clinics through Eucharistic procession and there are other cases throughout the country.

Remember, I am sending you out to be like sheep among wolves; you must be wary, then, as serpents, and yet innocent as doves.

Each one of the examples that I've listed is basically a single example of a set of criteria that I give. Since my conversion in 2008 I have consistently been asked, whether during my after talk Q&As, via email, phone calls or counseling… What, in my opinion, is the way to fight against abortion, how can we end the killing of babies in this way? The criteria I give is as follows:
Prayer and fasting.
Have an exorcism done on the property.
Have a priest do a Eucharistic procession with an image of our Lady of Guadalupe, and people following praying rosaries.
And have a mass said on the grounds.

I believe if people follow this criteria, we could shut down every abortion mill probably in the world.

So how about we look at an organization that HAS done this?

A Pro-life group out of Louisiana with a particular devotion to Our Lady of Guadalupe has shut down 25 abortion centers using these methods.

1 Corinthians 15:58
Stand firm, then, my beloved brethren, immovable in your resolve, doing your full share continually in the task the Lord has given you, since you know that your labor in the Lord's service cannot be spent in vain.

Has anyone ever heard of Jennifer McCoy?

She's a 43 year old married mother of 11. Who has been in the pro-life movement for 23 years.

Her entrance into her passionate involvement began and was inspired when she was 16 years old, after having an affair with her teacher, who was 23 years her senior she became pregnant. She had to leave her home because her mother was forcing her into an abortion, and she wanted to keep her child. At what was supposed to be her first checkup she was held down on the clinic table and the doctor proceeded to perform an abortion, when she tried to escape she was told that if she moved she could die from the procedure, she found out later that everyone in the clinic could hear her screaming and crying for help, but nobody came... later when she tried to take the clinic to court the judge told her that her mother had signed consent forms for the procedure, and as a minor there was nothing that she could do legally.

A few years ago, President Clinton passed the Rico act. It was basically an anti-conspiracy order, as a result a lot of Pro Life people were arrested and charged with RICO. In 1995 she was arrested and charged, found guilty at trial, and was sentenced 45 years. She had the support of Mother Theresa and Cardinal O'Connor. For her prolife views, she spent 2 and a half years of her sentence until the law was over turned. I thought a little back ground on our pro-life advocate was in order. Now for one more fun story. Several years later Jennifer and her baby son were in adoration. She felt Jesus gave her a message, so her, her young son, and her husband took a trip across this fair country of ours. The husband would stay in the car, and our other two warriors would visit Planned Parenthood, multiple Planned Parenthoods, in multiple states over the course of three months. The ploy? Mother and son would enter a planned parenthood posing as a mother who thinks she is now possibly pregnant and she went in for a pregnancy test... while inside and waiting her turn she would pass her young son around to the other expectant mothers, at almost every clinic at least one person would get up and leave with her. At one of these clinics there was a sign inside that said "no children allowed"... as she was walking in she noticed a young couple sitting outside on a bench, the young girl was holding an ultrasound of what looked like a 10 week old baby. Jennifer signed in inside, came back outside, and asked this young girl whom she didn't know and had never met, if she would hold her baby for her since no children were allowed inside. Jennifer walked back inside and pretended to wait. She came outside a few minutes later and the young expectant mother was playing with Jennifer's son and sobbing. Her and her boyfriend walked away with Jennifer and her son deciding to have the baby. In the course of 3 months Jennifer McCoy helped rescue over 100 babies from Planned Parenthood and certain death.

Remember, I am sending you out to be like sheep among wolves; you must be wary, then, as serpents, and yet innocent as doves.

Ephesians 5:15-17
"See then, brethren, how carefully you have to tread, not as fools, but as wise men do, hoarding the opportunity that is given you, in evil times like these. No, you cannot afford to be reckless; you must grasp what the Lord's will is for you."

Now, as I said earlier, I will give you my conversion story.

I would imagine that most people listening to this disc probably know something about my life. As of the typing up of the transcript of this disc my website currently has approximately 72,000 hits, so in theory

72,000 people know my story. We have a bunch of interviews all over the internet and on our website, and I'm an international speaker, so quite a few people have seen me live or have heard one of my talks online. But I understand that it's possible you may have bought this disc having never heard of Zachary King.

My testimony is approximately an hour long, what I want to share with you here, is what converted me. And then I'm going to tell you something that scares satan to death, something that he doesn't want me to tell you. But first, my conversion.

In January 2008 I worked at a place called piercing pagoda, in a mall in South Burlington Vermont. A woman named Mary Anne whom I had never met listened to the Holy Spirit, purchased something from my store, and had the nerve, and gall, to give me a blessed Miraculous Medal. Not knowing me, not knowing or even caring what my response would be, she just knew the Holy Spirit told her to and she was listening.

When she mentioned that "The Blessed Mother was calling me into her army" I had no idea who that was. My early years had been spent at the Baptist church. Mary gave birth to Jesus and that was that. When she told me that this miraculous medal was powerful, I had been at least neck deep, or probably most of the time, in way over my head, in Satanism, magick and the occult. So telling me something was powerful felt like a challenge, I knew that whatever this was it was in no way more powerful than me, and that it couldn't possibly have any affect. The Holy Spirit used my ego and my arrogance against me. I took it in my hand, ready to slam it on the counter or toss it on the floor, and let this woman know it was worthless. It holds no mystic, no power. I took it in my hand and clenched my fist, on doing so, my mall, and my store, disappeared. Everything was gone. I was standing in a darkened void with this woman Mary Ann standing in front of me. She told me that I had broken up a bunch of churches. I had helped commit over 100 abortions, had been practicing magick for over 25 years, and all of this was for the devil. That I was going to go to hell if I didn't change my ways. She was reading the scariest novel I had ever heard, and it was my life. She reiterated "The Blessed Mother was calling me into her army" and I knew in an instant that was the mother of God. It was an extremely strange revelation, for a former Baptist. In that moment, at that instant, Mary appeared to me. She took me by the hand and gently turned me around and her Son Jesus was standing behind me. To those that always asked, what does Jesus look like, in this manifestation He looked like a live version of the popular Divine Mercy Jesus. As if the artist had Jesus as an actual model. In that instant I knew everything Catholic was right, and Jesus was my Lord and Savior, and everything I had been doing, was wrong. My occult, and magick, came to a halt right there. And the Blessed

Mother told me that I was to help end abortion. Up until that time, I wanted to open my hand, but I was afraid to. I didn't know what would happen to me, I was afraid that I would fall through this darkened void forever and not find my way back, but I knew now that Jesus would not let me fall, or that if I fell Jesus would catch me. I will say that up until that moment, I thought that the only way to find any kind of happiness in this life was to seek temporal pleasure… I had wasted my entire life on hedonism… In this moment I found myself experiencing a holy love and peace. Things that I hadn't realize that I was missing, but that I had been so deeply hungry for, I had for so long sought happiness in things that never left me satiated, but instead sick with longing for more. It wasn't until I felt this fulfillment, this actual love, so different than anything I had ever experienced in my sad and sinful life, that I realized how broken I was, and that God wanted me, that God loved me as His own child ... I opened my hand and I was back in my mall in my store. And this woman Mary Ann was still talking to me. I learned where she went to mass, got the address, and I'll say the rest is history. If you want to know more, my website is Allsaintsministry.org.

Remember, I am sending you out to be like sheep among wolves; you must be wary, then, as serpents, and yet innocent as doves.

Within the world church of satan, and I would imagine some other satanic cults as well, it's well known things that satan is afraid of. I'll give you a hint. He attacks those things he's afraid of. Things that he knows can defeat him, he will attack with great ferocity. Want an example? GOD... What was the first battle in history? Satan vs God. Satan lost. Him and all his little helpers got kicked out of heaven. Now they're in control down here. What else does satan attack? Catholic church, he attacks us mightily. But I'm certain he's read that part in the bible that the Gates of Hell will not prevail, and he knows where he goes in the end. Now I know I said that I would reveal what he's scared to death of, and here's that part, also remember that the point of Part 3 is that this is spiritual warfare.

Satan has killed, murdered, 57,000,000+. That number only covers abortions in the United States since 1973 and abortions have been a part of human culture around the world since the beginning of time. Throughout history abortion has been wherever satan is, abortion, infanticide and satan are nearly synonymous Anthropologist Laila Williamson wrote that "Infanticide has been practiced on every continent and by people on every level of cultural complexity, from hunter gatherers to high civilizations, including our own ancestors. Rather than being an exception, then, it has been the rule." Most of the cases of abortion and infanticide have been done in the name of human sacrifice to pagan gods, whether it was the gods of the Aztecs, Moloch, or the Carthaginians burning their children in the name of

Baal Hamon… though there are plenty that killed for convenience such as the practices in Ancient Greece, there is even evidence of Paleolithic and Neolithic infanticide and cannibalism. Looking into the history of infanticide and abortion, it is very nearly exclusively only Judaism and Christianity that have held a consistent, passionate respect for the life of their children.

Abortion is a satanic sacrament, it is his favorite desecration.

Do you know how long God has known you?

Ephesians 1 verses 4 and 5 say He has chosen us out, in Christ, before the foundation of the world, to be saints, to be blameless in his sight, for love of him marking us out beforehand (so his will decreed) to be his adopted children through Jesus Christ.

There are so many atrocious things about abortion that satan loves… the emotional devastation, physical pain, death, the spilling of blood, the desecration of what is most beautiful and natural in the world, the greatest reflection of the Divine image in humanity… the love of a parent for their child…. But my theory is… that there is more than that to abortion. That satan is so hungry for abortion and the destruction of innocence, because he is terrified. He is terrified that we will realize that these children in the womb, with the help of their guardian angel, are able to act as prayer intercessors… the most pure, undefiled humans in existence… that these little humans are included when our Christ spoke at Matthew 18:10 saying, "See to it that you do not treat one of these little ones with contempt; I tell you, they have angels of their own in heaven, that behold the face of my heavenly Father continually."

Satan has such a hatred of innocence… so much of everything that he does is all rooted in the destruction of innocence. The prayers of the innocent, the unjaded, are the most powerful. If you can have a 3-5 year old pray for you, even if they don't know what exactly they are praying for, that is incredibly significant and effective.

Life begins at conception… at conception, the moment that we blink into existence, we are given our guardian angel. If these little children, the most undefiled of human life, when petitioned through their guardian angel, are able to communicate with God… to pray in whatever form God allows… would He not hear them?

I will quote again… for the last time… Matthew 10:16 "Remember, I am sending you out to be like sheep among wolves; you must be wary, then, as serpents, and yet innocent as doves."

Luke 1:39-55
In the days that followed, Mary rose up and went with all haste to a town of Juda, in the hill country where Zachary dwelt; and there entering in she gave Elizabeth

greeting. No sooner had Elizabeth heard Mary's greeting, than the child leaped in her womb; and Elizabeth herself was filled with the Holy Ghost; so that she cried out with a loud voice, Blessed art thou among women, and blessed is the fruit of thy womb. How have I deserved to be thus visited by the mother of my Lord? Why, as soon as ever the voice of thy greeting sounded in my ears, the child in my womb leaped for joy. Blessed art thou for thy believing; the message that was brought to thee from the Lord shall have fulfilment. And Mary said, my soul magnifies the Lord; my spirit has found joy in God, who is my Savior, because he has looked graciously upon the lowliness of his handmaid. Behold, from this day forward all generations will count me blessed; because he who is mighty, he whose name is holy, has wrought for me his wonders. He has mercy upon those who fear him, from generation to generation; he has done valiantly with the strength of his arm, driving the proud astray in the conceit of their hearts; he has put down the mighty from their seat, and exalted the lowly; he has filled the hungry with good things, and sent the rich away empty-handed. He has protected his servant Israel, keeping his merciful design in remembrance, according to the promise which he made to our forefathers, Abraham and his posterity for evermore.

This concludes part 3 of our set Abortion is a Satanic Sacrifice.

Original composition written and performed by Chris Johnson.

To contact Mr. Johnson he can be reached via email at tompop71@gmail.com

Thank you for listening to the information, and we want to give a huge shout out to the Blessed Mother for rescuing me and for being a truly perfect mother to all of us.

Observation Number One

Insanity: doing the same thing over and over again and expecting different results.

~ Albert Einstein

In the prolife movement we write laws every year and we march every year and abortion is still legal. Why haven't we learned? Abortion is spiritual warfare. How we fight the abortion war is the definition of insanity.

Observation Number Two

In 2004 a group of pro-life activists started a tradition of fasting and prayer outside of an abortion clinic in Bryan Texas over the course of 40 days. As of 2013, that first abortion mill in Bryan Texas, shut down.

I am not knocking 40 Days for Life. When they started they were about the only game in town. Having been a satanist for so long, and recognizing the rules of spiritual warfare, I think something needs to be pointed out. It took 9 years to shut down this first clinic. People prayed and fasted 40 days a year for 9 years. How many days is that? 360 days. How many days are in a year? 365 days. To me it sounds like God is saying, "If you would have fasted for one year, I would have shut down the clinic." We are the ones that chose to pray for 9 years, He shut it down in 360 days. Maybe we should learn this lesson. I'm just saying.

Observation Number Three

As a High Wizard I committed the mortal sin of assisting at 146 abortions. I would have had 149, but 3 of them failed. Here is the story of one of those failures.

Most abortions are done at night. Most of mine were not done in an actual abortion clinic but approximately 20 were. Three of those 20 did not work properly.

I arrived during the day with a group of Satanists. On our side of the street was a satanic biker gang who were gesturing rudely and grabbing their crotches, baring their breasts and butts to the people across the street. The bikers were cussing them out, smoking cigarettes and flicking the cigarettes at the people. The people across the street were very quiet and many had their eyes closed. The people were holding some kind of prayer rope or chain; I did not know exactly what they had in their hands. All of the people seemed to have one. I walked inside with my entourage the abortion was going to be on the second floor. The second floor has large windows and from there we could hear chanting from across the street. The entourage is in the room with the abortion doctor and nurse and they are prepping the woman. I am standing by the windows with my friend when I noticed that the people across the street are now kneeling, they are all holding these prayer ropes and they are chanting something that we can't quite make out. As satanists we chanted. The windows in the room open via a crank. I opened the windows and I repeated what I was hearing. I heard, "Hail Mary full of Grace the Lord is with thee, blessed art though among women and blessed is the fruit of thou womb Jesus." My friend then repeated what he was hearing "Holy Mary Mother of God pray for us sinners now and at the hour of our death". We looked at each other and laughed. I then closed the windows as the chanting continued the doctor said we were almost ready so I prepped myself, gloves and a surgical mask. As noted earlier in this transcript my job, as the main magick practitioner, is to get blood on my hands. It does not matter if it is the woman's or the baby's. The doctor became slightly indignant when he discovered the woman wasn't dilated yet as she apparently had already been prepped and should have been ready at this time. As a side note here, this was approximately her 10th abortion. This was a late term abortion. She was a "breeder". Breeders intentionally get pregnant for the purpose of aborting their children. The woman became very upset as she said the baby was in the birth canal. She got into an argument with the doctor who informed her that he was a doctor and the baby was not in the birth canal. She was very insistent and asked me if it was also my first rodeo. I told her I was not a doctor and could not really answer any of her questions. A few minutes passed while the doctor and I chatted and the woman continually cussed us both. The doctor checked one more time. He said we were all wasting our time being there we should reschedule for another time or possibly another day. As he said the last couple of words, we heard a baby cry. We looked down and the baby had come out, the doctor had just checked, there is no way the baby went from the womb to outside that woman in a few seconds. Remember, she was not dilated. When this event occurs, there is an attorney a nurse and a social worker that come into the room and take over. The baby is almost instantly adopted usually by a good family, not satanists, but someone who actually wants the child. As a High Wizard, we had to write reports on every spell and ritual. As I had three of these failures, I asked to see all of the other Wizards failed attempts at abortion. I wanted to know if there was a common denominator. Every failure took place during the day during the normal business hours of the abortion clinics. Every failure took place with people nearby praying on prayer ropes, prayer beads, worry chain, or some other similar name. No one ever called it a rosary. I never figured out that Mary was stopping my abortion attempts until I became Catholic. Never be ashamed to pray your rosary, especially at the abortion clinic.

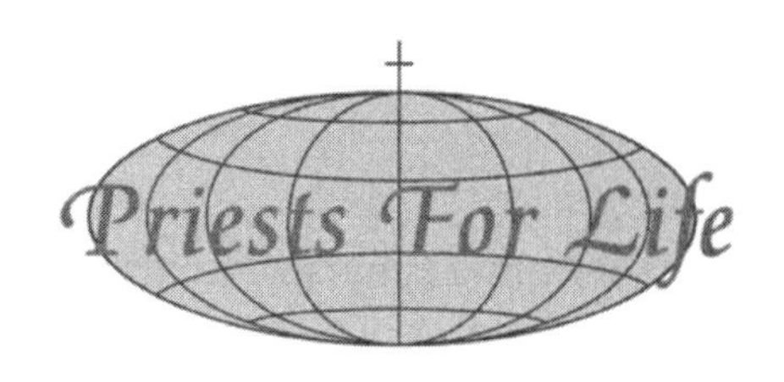

Activating the Church to End Abortion

April 3, 2017

To whom it may concern:

For the past several years I have known Mr. Zachary King, and have been impressed by his testimony of how God rescued him from the kingdom of darkness and brought him into the Kingdom of Light, from the service of Satan to the service of the true God, and from supporting abortion to supporting the protection of every life, born and unborn.

I praise God for Zachary's testimony and urge everyone to listen to it! For those who serve the Lord, it will be a blessing of encouragement; for those unsure of their path in life, it will be a guiding light and for those still trapped in darkness, it will be a clear summons to come to Christ!

My prayer is that both Zachary, and all who hear his story, will enjoy the fullness of God's protection and life!

Sincerely,

Fr. Frank Pavone

Fr. Frank Pavone
National Director, Priests for Life
President, National Pro-life Religious Council